# DEAR OWNER

YOU, YOUR DOG, AND EVERYTHING NO ONE TOLD YOU

BETHANY JOHNSON

*For my dad, Joe Mangascle. I've got my cup of Joe - I'll wait for you to get yours.*

*I love you forever.*

**Copyright © 2025 Bethany Johnson**

All rights reserved. No part of this publication may be reproduced, distributed, or transmitted in any form or by any means, including photocopying, recording, or other electronic or mechanical methods, without the prior written permission of the publisher, except in the case of brief quotations embodied in critical reviews and certain other noncommercial uses permitted by copyright law.

First Edition, 2025

Published by Walking Dog Company, LLC

ISBN (Paperback): 979-8-9999963-0-5

ISBN (ebook): 979-8-9999963-1-2

This book is based on the author's personal experiences. It is not intended as a substitute for professional veterinary or medical advice. Readers are encouraged to consult a qualified professional for guidance specific to their situation.

Cover design by Grace Perdana Mulia

## INTRODUCTION

If you're holding this book, there's a good chance you didn't get the dog you imagined.

You know - the one who would sleep at your feet, greet strangers politely, and never make you feel like you're doing everything wrong.

Instead, you got *this* dog.

The one who barks at your neighbor's mailbox. The one who has made you cry in your car after a walk. The one who has you Googling "is it normal to regret getting a dog" at 1 a.m.

I wrote this book because I've been there - more than once. I know what it's like to wonder if you're cut out for this, to feel like every other owner is doing it better, and to scroll through training advice until you're overwhelmed and convinced your dog is broken (or you are).

Over the past eight years of working closely with dog owners, I've noticed something - no matter the breed, the training method, or the "issue," the conversations almost always circle back to us. To the stories we tell ourselves. To the insecurities we've carried around for years. Getting a challenging dog has a way of bringing all of that to the surface - the people pleasing, the second-guessing, the fear of being seen or looking like you have no idea what you're doing. And before you know it, you realize it's not just about training your dog anymore. It's about showing up differently - for them, and for you.

That's also why I'm here, writing this. When my dad passed away in 2023, I couldn't stop thinking about how he'd always wanted to write a book. So now, it feels like we're doing it together. He had this way of telling stories that made you lean in - the kind you'd think about days later without even meaning to. We talked about writing something together one day, but we ran out of time. Losing him made me realize how easy it is to put off the things that matter most until "someday." So here I am, doing the thing. For him. For me. And maybe as your sign to stop waiting, too.

So, Dear Owner - this isn't a step-by-step training manual.

It's a collection of stories, lessons, and the kind of hard-earned truths I wish someone had told me sooner. It's about your dog, yes - but it's also about you. About how this unexpected challenge might be the thing that changes you in ways you didn't see coming.

You won't find quick fixes or sugarcoated advice in here. You'll find the messy middle, the slow wins, and the little glimmers that remind you it's working - even if no one else notices.

Getting a dog who challenges you doesn't mean you did something wrong. Sometimes, that dog is the one who ends up changing everything.

I didn't get the dog that fit into my life.

I got the dog that changed it.

# Part One: The Unexpected

## 1 / CRYING ON THE FLOOR

What did we do?

I'm lying on our bedroom floor. Annoyed at the linoleum. The orange hue irritates me.

In the other room, our new puppy whines in his kennel.

The older dogs hate him.

I'm not even sure *I* like him.

This is all my fault.

Bobby glances toward the kennel. "Maybe we should take him back to the shelter."

I hated those words. They felt like giving up.

But he's probably right.

It's not supposed to feel this hard - is it?

"I'll try to figure it out," I said. "Let's give it one more day."

The truth?

I wanted to take him back too.

As much as I hated the thought of it.

This new dog felt like an intruder.

Like a mistake.

So, I got a dog - because what I really wanted was a baby.

But I can't get pregnant.

And now? I can't even get the dog thing right.

Perfect.

When Bobby left, I stayed on the floor.

Worried and tired.

What if I have no idea what I'm doing?

What if he's right?

Can I really make this better?

I took off for my first dog walk of the day. A doodle named Jerry.

He pulled so hard I started rollerblading with him instead of walking.

Earbuds in. YouTube open.

Frantically searching:

"Dog training help."

"What if I don't like my dog?"

"Our dogs hate the puppy - please help."

I stumbled upon a dog trainer duo whose videos felt like I was sitting in their living room – new friends hanging out.

Dog training had always seemed so intimidating.

But they made it feel... cool?

Like listening to them made me excited to start training. And the way they talked about the hard stuff - the pushy, anxious, overwhelming dogs - I was excited to try some of the things with our new dog Theo.

All day long, they buzzed in my ears while I went from one house to the next. In one video, they mentioned a seminar they hosted for aspiring trainers.

I was a dog walker at the time, unsure of my next step.

And suddenly, something clicked.

I'd been running my pet sitting business for the past few years and loved the dogs I worked with.

But something was missing.

Purpose. Direction.

Something to feel proud of.

And with this new idea - *what if I could be a dog trainer?* - I started testing things out with Theo.

I tried the suggestions from the videos.

And slowly, I started to see changes.

Maybe he's not the dog I expected.

But he might be the one who changes everything.

Our new puppy, Theo.

## 2 / MY DOG WHISPERER ERA

My least favorite part of school dances was when the slow songs started. That awkward panic, knowing no one was going to ask me to dance - just standing there, wishing I could disappear into the wall.

That's kind of what it feels like to have a dog that doesn't really *fit in*. The one you have to warn people about before they come over. The dog you're never really sure how to explain. The one that makes you feel like you don't belong in the story you thought you were signing up for: *Get a dog - it'll be great!*

But when you get a dog who's reactive, anxious, or barks nonstop at a stranger who's just trying to get their mail, you start to wonder: What the hell did I get myself into? And am I the only one?

My first experience with a dog who made me question everything was our girl Sadie. She was a shepherd/lab mix, and right around six months old, she started pushing boundaries in that subtle-but-relentless way that makes you wonder if you're *actually* in charge.

One day, I was lying in bed, when she walked up to me - and growled.

Excuse me? This was new.

I froze. I had no idea what it meant or what I was supposed to do - so, naturally, I turned to Google.

"What to do when you think your dog might be planning your murder?"

Okay, that's not exactly what I typed... but you get the vibe.

That search led me to Cesar Milan. Enter: my Dog Whisperer era. I binged every episode like my life depended on it. I wanted so badly to be the calm, assertive pack leader he talked about and studied his moves like I was cramming for a final exam.

One technique I saw over and over was the "calm surrender" - gently guiding the dog onto their side to help them relax and "submit" to leadership. It looked peaceful. Empowering. Totally doable.

So naturally, I decided to try it.

I took Sadie into the backyard feeling like I was about to film my own episode.

I told her to lie down.

She didn't.

So I tried to help her lie down.

She resisted.

So I did what any overcommitted, underqualified pack leader might do - I awkwardly got on top of her and used my body weight to keep her down.

It was less "calm surrender" and more "panicked backyard wrestling." By the end, I was panting. My hair was stuck to my face. Sadie was very much not surrendered - just confused and mildly offended.

That day taught me something I didn't understand yet: Sadie wasn't a bad dog. She was just... figuring me out. And honestly, I was figuring her out too. That's one of the things nobody talks about when you get a dog. Sometimes it's not instantly great. Sometimes it's chaotic and unnerving.

Some dogs flow with you. Some challenge you. And some - if you're lucky - do both.

My first dog teacher, Sadie May

## 3 / EXPECTATIONS

I bought a bird feeder because I wanted to be a person who watches birds.

You know the kind. The type who drinks her morning coffee wrapped in a blanket, looking serene and slightly windswept, while chickadees flutter in the sunlight and a breeze drifts gently through the trees.

I imagined myself in a mountain cottage. Peace. Connection. Maybe a deer wandering by to nod in approval.

What I got was squirrels.

Squirrels who ransacked the feeder, flung seed all over the patio like they were hosting an unhinged buffet, and invited every bird in a 30-mile radius to participate in what I can only describe as a full-scale seed war.

And of course - because life is funny - my dogs started eating the birdseed.

Which gave them diarrhea.

Which gave me a new morning routine of *"coffee + cleaning up regrets."*

The bird feeder had to go.

I stood at the back window one morning watching a squirrel dangle upside down from the feeder, seed raining down like confetti, and thought - *this was supposed to be peaceful*.

But that's the thing about expectations. They rarely match up with reality. Especially the romanticized ones.


When we picture dog ownership, it usually looks something like this:

- "My dog will be my best friend."

- "We'll go on calm walks together every day."

- "Training will be easy - they're smart!"

- "My dog will love everyone."

- "What worked with my last dog will work with her."

- "They'll grow out of it."

- "We'll be that chill dog + owner duo at the brewery or park."


What we don't picture is barking at delivery trucks, leash reactivity, chewed furniture, nervous systems shot from constant whining, or crying in the car outside the vet's office because *why is my dog like this*.

And just like the bird feeder - I'm not saying it's all bad.

But it's rarely what we expected.

And sometimes the gap between the dream and the reality is where the real work begins.

It's not about giving up on the vision - it's about letting it evolve.

Because when reality doesn't match the story we told ourselves, we have two choices: cling tighter... or rewrite the story.

Here are a few of the most common expectations I've seen (and believed myself) and the gentler, more grounded versions I've come to learn along the way:

- Instead of: "My dog will be my best friend right away." → "Our bond might take time - and that's okay. Trust is built, not instant."
- Instead of: "We'll go on peaceful walks together every day." → "Walks might be a work in progress, but each one gives us a chance to practice and grow."
- Instead of: "Training will be easy - they're smart!" → "Training is a journey, and my dog's cleverness means I get to meet them where they are - with patience and strategy."
- Instead of: "My dog will love everyone." → "My dog doesn't need to love everyone - they just need to feel safe and understood."
- Instead of: "As long as I love them enough, they'll turn out great." → "Love is the foundation - but structure, advocacy, and training help love go further."

- Instead of: "They'll grow out of it." → "Growth takes guidance. With support, my dog can learn how to navigate the world."
- Instead of: "We'll be that chill dog + owner duo at the brewery or park." → "We may not be 'that duo' - but we're building a relationship that feels good for us."
- Instead of: "My dog won't need the crate." → "A crate isn't punishment - it's a tool to help my dog feel secure and supported."

You don't need to have it all figured out. Just start noticing the stories you've been telling yourself - about your dog, about you - and see which ones are *actually* worth keeping.

And maybe the bird feeder wasn't a total fail. It was just a reminder that expectations almost never play out the way we want. And that's not always bad. With dogs (and life), it's usually the messy version that ends up meaning more anyway.

Maybe your dog wasn't sent to test you - maybe they were sent to teach you what you're capable of.

## 4 / THE SEASONS YOU DON'T EXPECT

THERE ARE moments in life that split everything into "before" and "after." Losing my dad was one of them.

I'm in the hospital room. Same one we've been in all week.

My mom called earlier. Said it was time.

Dad is gone.

My brother is sitting at the end of the bed. I'm a few feet away. My mom is closest, holding my dad's hands.

I try to stand but my knees buckle. I collapse halfway, sobbing. The kind of crying where you can't breathe, no matter how hard you try. Like it hit me all at once - he's gone.

My mom pulls me in, comforting in that way only moms can. Then my brother gets up and wraps his arms around both of us.

The crying stops.

And for a moment, I think - maybe I'll be okay.

A year has passed, and I feel anxious. The holidays are approaching and they're the hardest for me. My dad was such a big presence and now it's all I notice when I'm at their house - he's not here.

The grief always finds me.

And underneath the sadness, I'm angry.

Angry that Bobby's parents are still alive.

And then ashamed, because what kind of person thinks like that?

I go through phases. One day I'm embracing grief like it's a new friend. I give myself "grief days" and stay in bed watching *This Is Us* reruns - finding a strange comfort in seeing TV characters go through something similar.

And then the next day, I beat myself up for not getting over it yet.

Grief is the most disorienting thing I've ever experienced and it shows up when I least expect it. Usually when I'm driving and a song comes on that reminds me of him - of loss and love.

It's something I never could have prepared for. No book, podcast, or therapy session could make the process easier. It's just something I've learned to live with. The ups, the downs, and everything in between.

And in a strange way, that's not so different from what it feels like to bring a dog into your life. Sometimes it feels like you're moving through seasons you never planned for - ones that shift and change before you've even figured out the last one.

Here's what that can look like:

**Turn 1: The Hoping Phase**

"This is just a phase. He'll grow out of it."

You tell yourself it's normal. That all dogs act like this sometimes. You keep waiting for the "real" version of your dog to appear - the one you imagined when you first brought them home.

**Turn 2: The Frustration Phase**

"Why is this so hard? Why can't my dog be more normal?"

The irritability sets in - with your dog, with yourself, with every happy dog-and-owner pair you pass on the street. You cry during walks. You dread getting the leash out.

**Turn 3: The If-I-Just Phase**

"Maybe if I just use more food... maybe if I just exercise him more..."

This is the late-night Googling era. You're looking for the magic button. The one perfect solution that will turn your dog into the dream version in your head.

**Turn 4: The Heavy Phase**

"Maybe I'm not cut out for this."

The isolation creeps in. The shame, too - because it feels

awful to admit you don't love your dog the way you thought you would.

**Turn 5: The Settling-In Phase**

"This is the dog I have. And I'm going to learn how to help her, even if it looks different than I imagined."

This isn't giving up. It's shifting from chasing the dream dog to showing up for the dog in front of you. It's not instantly harmonious, but it's when the doubt quiets just enough for you to think, maybe I can actually do this.

Maybe you're somewhere in these turns right now.

Or maybe you've already made it through them and can only see it clearly in hindsight.

Either way, nothing about this makes you a bad owner.

It just means you're in the thick of it - the part every dog owner goes through in some way, even if they don't always talk about it.

And if you recognize yourself here, you'll probably recognize a lot of what's ahead - the messy, real-life moments and the small shifts that help you find your way through. The same way grief slowly teaches you how to keep going, dogs have a way of shaping you in the middle of it all - pulling you through the hard parts toward something you didn't know you were capable of.

I hope you know you can be both a mess and a really, *really* good dog owner.

## 5 / PERFECTIONISM

CAN I SUCK YOUR TOES?

I'm sitting in a navy-blue cloth chair, legs draped over one side, while the sounds of WrestleMania echo from a TV in the corner.

I'm in the psych ward. I was admitted a few hours ago.

A part of me was relieved to be there. To get out of the disaster of a life I'd been trying (and failing) to hold together. Everything I was avoiding had finally caught up with me, and here I was.

On my left is a large man, watching the wrestling match like it's the Super Bowl. On my right, a smaller woman working on a puzzle. She doesn't say much, but she *does* happen to look exactly like Chucky from the horror movies. Which... feels like a choice.

And then -

"Can I suck your toes?" the large man asks.

Now, you'd think this would be the moment I screamed. But for some reason, it didn't feel out of place.

I mean, sure, I'd never been asked that before. But in the psych ward? Honestly, it tracked.

So instead of panic, my brain calmly went with: *No, thank you.*

Like it was just part of the program. Like next, the Chucky-lookalike might ask me to reenact a horror scene with her, and I'd probably shrug and say, *Yeah, okay.*

I wish I could say I laughed it off, but the truth is, I didn't feel much of anything. My body was there, but my brain was hovering somewhere above me, like a drone camera just watching the scene unfold.

I'd hit that point where life stops feeling like your own. Where you're technically in the room, but the mess in your head is so loud that everything else feels like background noise.

So when the man asked about my toes, it barely registered. Like - sure. Add it to the list of things I didn't know how to deal with. Right behind: Why am I like this? and How the hell did I end up here?

The Chucky-lookalike woman slid another puzzle piece into place. No comment. No reaction. Like *this* was just another Tuesday to her. And maybe it was.

Me? I felt the weight of my parents sitting at home, probably wondering if they did the right thing. Wondering how to explain this to people without feeling like they failed as parents. I hated knowing they were scared for me.

But also - relief.

Relief that I wasn't in charge for once.

Relief that someone else was going to have to figure out if I needed meds, or therapy, or just a padded room where people asked about my toes instead of my GPA or career path.

It's weird to say, but in that moment, the psych ward didn't feel like rock bottom. It felt like a pause button. A break from pretending everything was fine when it absolutely wasn't.

And maybe that's what I needed most.

A pause.

A timeout before life swallowed me whole.

It's strange, but that night in the psych ward was the first time I realized how much pressure I'd been carrying to keep it all together. To be the girl who looked fine on the outside, even when the inside was a disaster zone.

And that's the thing about perfectionism - it doesn't always show up as wanting straight A's or having a spotless home. Sometimes it's just the constant pretending. The keeping it together so nobody notices you're unraveling.

And perfectionism doesn't stop with you. When you're a dog owner, it shows up in the sneakiest of ways:

• Replaying every mistake - like your dog barking at the neighbor and you still cringe about it days later.

• Avoiding busy walking times because you don't want an audience if your dog loses it.

- Over-prepping - stuffing your pockets with every tool and treat just so you feel "ready."

- Comparing your dog to every calm golden retriever you pass on the street.

- Skipping over the wins because you're focused on what's still not working.

- Hesitating to try new things - because if it's not perfect, why even bother?

My dad used to say the mind is negatively biased.

Meaning, our thoughts are wired to lean toward the worst-case scenario.

I'm not enough.

Nobody likes me.

Someone else would do this better.

And if you follow that storyline long enough, it feels almost impossible to believe any other version of yourself.

Which is why I think it hits so hard when you get a dog who's challenging.

Because suddenly, that negative narrative you've been carrying your whole life?

Your dog starts to feel like the proof.

I struggled with this for a long time, because I saw my dogs as an *extension* of myself.

How they behaved felt like a direct reflection of how good - or how bad - I was.

For me, it was all about control - the endless game of trying to manage how I came across to everyone else.

Flattering angles in pictures.

Wearing clothes that make you look thinner.

Talking less so you don't say the "wrong" thing.

It never ends.

My entire life's been shaped by the question: What will they think of me?

So, when I got a dog who felt chaotic - who didn't match the polished, happy image I had in my head - it was like being confronted with everything I tried to hide.

But here's the thing about dogs:

You can't beg them to snap out of it.

You can't plead with them to stop lunging and barking on walks just because it's embarrassing.

This is a narrative you can't control.

And maybe that's the gift.

Because when you can't control the story anymore, you finally have a chance to rewrite it.

Not into something perfect - but into something real.

Something honest.

One that lets you show up messy, human, and still worthy of whatever the hell you want.

Sometimes I think back to that night in the psych ward - how lost I felt, how sure I was that being broken meant being unworthy. And maybe that's why I love working with messy dogs so much now. Because I know what it's like to need someone who won't give up on you just because you're hard to handle.

## 6 / WHERE NERVOUS DOGS BLOOM

"Nobody's ever walked her before," said Olive's owner, her voice cracking - part disbelief, part *holy crap, maybe we'll be okay.*

NERVOUS DOGS ARE my favorite to work with.

It hasn't always been that way, but over the years they've taught me how to slow down and pay attention to the small stuff.

Things I'm not very good at. I'm more of a steamroll- past-the-details because I'm already onto the next thing kind of girl.

But the more nervous dogs I work with, the clearer it gets that a small moment can change everything.

And Olive was the first dog that really solidified that for me.

. . .

When her owner reached out, her intake form said:

**"Extremely fearful of people. Barking. Cowering. May run toward the door."**

It's the kind of form that makes you pause, because you know you're meeting a dog who's carrying a lot - and an owner who's probably carrying just as much.

Most dogs on drop off day will jump on me or get really wiggly at the sight of a new person. And some might bark if they're more nervous around someone new. Olive wanted to stay away from me - not in a panicked way. She was more like, "no thank you, I don't need more people in my life." Honestly? Same, Olive. Same.

I couldn't sense any aggression or timidness that would make me think she might bite, so I walked with the owner to see how she'd respond to me if I walked with them.

A big part of working with dogs like Olive is I basically ignore them during that first intro. And this is because dogs feed off of energy. This isn't a "woo-woo" kind of thing - it's just most dogs get excited when the human is excited. Kind of makes sense. (If only that also worked on husbands when you're excited about adding a few more garden beds he now has to build.)

So with a dog like Olive who's nervous of people, I stay a little boring on purpose. No big moves, no high-pitched voice - just calm and predictable.

I kept my attention on the owner, not Olive, and walked her through how to hand over the leash. "Don't make a big deal out of it," I told her. "Just pass it to me and keep walking." No pep talks. No dramatic pause. Just a quiet switch.

What I really wanted to see was how Olive would handle realizing that I was the one holding the leash now - no pressure, just me stepping into her space without forcing it.

Once we got through that hand-off without any drama, I knew we had something to build on. So I took Olive into my backyard and sat by the pool. No talking. No trying to get her to like me with words. Just trying to help her feel safe by doing nothing.

The best way to describe it is primal.

If you think about it - dogs can't talk. But we *love* talking to them.

And there's nothing wrong with that. I have full-on conversations with my dog Johnny every day and it brings me so much joy.

But with a new dog who's cautious of people? It's different.

So I just sat - and after about 20 minutes, Olive laid down. Not next to me, but a few feet away.

I held her leash loosely, just in case she got spooked and tried to bolt. No tension. Just a safety net.

Over the next few days, I hand-fed her meals.

I'd sit calmly by her kennel, offer a piece of food in my hand, and wait.

If she didn't take it, I'd toss it gently toward her.

Still no talking - maybe a soft "good" every now and then.

Sometimes I'd put on headphones and listen to music that made me feel calm or grounded.

Movie soundtracks or Christmas oldies are always my go-to.

Because sometimes - okay, a lot of the time - it's not just about the dog.

It's about you.

You don't have to be perfectly calm or in the right mindset every second. (If that were a requirement, I would've been fired from my own job years ago.)

But the more you pay attention to how *you're* feeling - and find ways to re-center yourself - the easier it is to see progress.

Because when you're grounded, you notice the good stuff. But when you're stressed and overwhelmed? You'll find more reasons to stay there.


A few days into working with Olive, I sat on a couch on our back porch. She dragged a leash around as she sniffed about - investigating new smells.

And then after about five minutes of doing her own thing, she walked over, sat beside me and laid her head on the couch.

One of those small-big moments that can change everything for a nervous dog. Because when a nervous dog finds a safe place to land - it gets a little easier to show them that the world might not be so scary after all.

So if you're sitting there with a nervous dog, wondering if it'll ever feel easier - don't dismiss the small stuff. A glance your way. A softer tail. Choosing to sit near you instead of hiding. Those things aren't insignificant. They're proof that it's working. And little by little, they add up to the kind of change you've been hoping for.

There are four principles I always come back to when working with nervous dogs. They're the anchors that keep me steady when progress feels slow, and the reminders I lean on when I start to overthink or wonder if I'm doing enough.

## 1 - Talk less, move more.

One of the reasons I love working with nervous dogs so much is that they force me to slow down. In a world that feels busy and distracting, they're like a break from the noise. Most nervous dogs are already overstimulated by sounds, movement, and energy - so the best thing you can do is not add to it. Try noticing how much you're talking to your dog, and experiment with only saying what's necessary. It's harder than it sounds, but it makes a difference.

## 2 - Don't get stuck in the story.

Sometimes a dog's past matters, but more often, it keeps us spinning in circles instead of moving forward. Nervous dogs don't sit around reliving their history the way we do. They live in the now - which is why your dog acts like you've been gone for years when you only ran to the mailbox. If you want to help a nervous dog build confidence, do what they do: focus on today, and what's possible right now.

## 3 - Consistency wins every time.

The fastest way to give a nervous dog confidence? Make life predictable. Keep your routines simple and repeatable. Feed them around the same times. Stick with training habits, even if they're small. Nervous dogs thrive when they know what to expect - it makes the world feel less overwhelming. Missing a day won't ruin everything, but the steadier you are, the more they'll relax.

## 4 - When in doubt, clip on the leash.

A leash isn't just a tool - it's reassurance and support. For a nervous dog, having that tether can help them feel like they're not out there on their own, especially in moments when they freeze or panic. It gives you a way to guide them instead of leaving them to figure it out on their own. Think of it less like a restriction and more like a lifeline that says, *"I've got you."*

So if you have a nervous dog, keep this close: the little things *do* matter. Every calm handoff, every quiet moment, every leash clipped on when you're not sure what else to do - those are wins. They might not look flashy to anyone else, but your dog feels them. And over time, those tiny steps stack up. Nervous dogs don't transform overnight, but they do transform. And when they do, it's because you showed up for them in the slow, steady, boring ways that no one claps for - like the dog-training version of brushing your teeth. Nobody's handing you a trophy, but one day you wake up and realize: hey, this actually worked.

## 7 / PEOPLE PLEASING

Everything inside me screamed - GO GET HIM.

Before Theo, the game plan was nursing school. The reliable route.

Until one day I cut my finger (a small cut, mind you) while slicing peppers - and almost passed out. Not because there was a lot of blood, but because the sight of it made me nauseous.

So, yeah... probably time to rethink the whole nursing thing.

At some point, I started thinking about jobs I might actually enjoy. I loved hanging out with my dogs, but my grades weren't exactly vet school material. So I turned to the internet and searched for "dogs with jobs". When I saw 'dog trainer' in the results, it felt like a breadcrumb I was supposed to follow.

After watching way too many *Dog Whisperer* episodes and unsuccessfully trying a few things with Sadie, I was curious.

Could I really be a dog trainer?? Is that... a thing people without a TV show actually do?

(Funny to think about now - I was drawn to dog training before I ever got Theo.)

Curious to see if this was actually something I could do, I emailed five businesses in the area, hoping someone would let me learn from them - and Sam was the only one who replied.

"Can you get here at 2?"

He was an older, gruff guy who coached football part-time. I started going on one-on-one sessions with him - and one Saturday, I brought my dog Charlie.

He's always been the calm, go-with-the-flow type who loves everyone, and I knew he'd be a good distraction.

I drove over in my white Nissan Sentra, windows down, Charlie's nose wet from all the smells. When we pulled up, Sam asked me to keep Charlie in the car while we went inside to meet the owners and talk.

We've done this plenty of times before.

I left the car running with the AC blasting. Charlie stretched out in the backseat. He knew the drill - I'd be right back.

Inside, we sat on the couch, talking with the owners about their dog - how tough the walks were, how overwhelmed they felt - and Sam reassuring them about his plan to help. About ten minutes in, I glanced out the window toward my car and saw Charlie looking back at me.

Sitting up.

Panting.

Even though I'd left the AC on.

That's strange.

"Um, excuse me," I interrupted Sam mid-sentence. "I think I need to go get Charlie. He's panting in the car even though the AC's on."

"Oh, I'm sure he's fine," Sam said, trying to wave it off and keep the session on track.

But everything inside me screamed - GO GET HIM.

And in that moment, I almost let my people-pleasing instincts win. I almost stayed quiet. Careful to not seem rude.

And if I had, my life would've changed forever.

But in that moment, my fears got the best of me and I got up to go check. As I got closer to the car, full panic set in.

I opened the door and a wall of hot air hit my face.

**THE AC WAS BLOWING HOT AIR. OH MY GOD.**

I pulled Charlie out and his body was limp. Sam rushed over, grabbed a hose, and we started cooling him off. We sat outside for what felt like forever, waiting and hoping. Charlie started to perk up and seemed ok. But I wasn't.

I cried the whole way home. Mad that I hesitated. Angry at my old stupid car with its garbage AC. But mostly mad at myself - for almost letting my fear of upsetting someone keep me from going out to check on him.

That moment with Charlie was extreme, but people-pleasing shows up in so many ways. Like letting your family feed your dog scraps even though you've asked them not to. Or standing there awkwardly while someone pets your dog, even though you really don't want them to - but you also don't want to be "that owner."

It doesn't always feel like a big deal in the moment, but it chips away at your confidence - especially when your dog's depending on you to speak up. As much as I'd love to say that day changed me - that I never second-guessed myself again - it didn't. I still had a lot of learning and unlearning left to do. Lessons that wouldn't just come from dogs - but from life, loss, and all the things I never saw coming.

My sweet boy, Charlie.

Learning to advocate for your dog is often the first time you learn to advocate for yourself.

# 8 / MUSIC

WE ALL HAVE something that shaped how we process the world.

For some people, it's books. For others, sports.

For me - it was music.

And if I had to guess, it's probably why I feel so deeply about dogs. Because music taught me how to really feel things - even the hard stuff.

It's also what helps me *not* overreact when I'm working with a dog who's wound tight. I've learned that the calmer I am, the calmer they are - so if that means putting on Christmas oldies in July while an anxious dog paces the room, then Bing Crosby and I are spending the afternoon together. Sometimes it's Taylor Swift - bright, steady, easy to hum along to - when I'm helping a nervous dog learn to walk beside me. Other times it's Bon Iver when I'm working with a pushy dog who makes me want to match their energy (but shouldn't). The right song slows my breathing, softens my tone, and keeps me grounded - and dogs notice that. They might not understand the music, but they understand *me* in that moment. And that changes everything.

Growing up, I loved music. Especially the soundtracks of movies.

I still remember road trips with my parents - headphones on, CD player humming, usually something moody like the Garden State soundtrack.

I'd stare out the window, imagining myself as the lead in a movie.

Depending on the song, I was either wildly misunderstood or about to fall in love. I was pretty much always pretending that I was the girl being chased by the boy - probably because it was the complete opposite of my actual life.

Some kids disappeared into books - me?

I vanished into music.

I got into basketball when I was in middle school. I was tall and sturdy enough to be good at it, even though everywhere else in my life I wanted to be smaller.

Some of my favorite memories were car rides with my dad after games. And the music was always a soundtrack. Our favorite was The Last of the Mohicans (his pick). We'd sit in silence as it played, each scene moving from quiet intros to epic war scenes. Somehow, the music said more than either of us needed to.

My mom always played old musicals in the house, which is probably why I still listen to classic Christmas music year-round. The voices of Nat King Cole and Frank Sinatra feel like a nervous system reset - especially when I'm working with a challenging or anxious dog. I put my headphones on and their voices become my anchor - pulling me out of the chaos and back to something steady.

But music became something different when my dad went into the hospital.

We knew things weren't getting any better and my mom had been staying with him every night - but one night I offered to give her a break and stay in her place. I thought I'd be okay. But sitting in that hospital room alone, I didn't know what to do. So I did the only thing that made sense - I turned to music.

I played the soundtrack from Road to Perdition - one of my dad's favorite movies - and then The Last of the Mohicans. I held my phone to his ear and whispered stories into the room, hoping the music would do what I couldn't. I held his hands, studying them - trying to memorize each line so I wouldn't forget.

Each morning before heading back to the hospital, I'd try to make myself look somewhat decent — straightening my hair while listening to the Doobie Brothers. Their music wasn't something I regularly listened to, but something about them reminded me of him. I craved older male energy. Strength and steadiness. I listened to the same five songs on repeat, disappearing into a world that didn't include a hospital bed.

In high school, I actually saw them live. My parents weren't the concert-going type, but that day we went downtown to see the Doobie Brothers. There was someone smoking a blunt behind us (a fact I found funny and scandalous as a sophomore in high school), but the day stuck with me.

A few weeks later, my mom and I drove around town on the 4th of July looking for fireworks - the Doobie Brothers playing the whole way.

So now, when I hear their music, it doesn't just feel like a song. It feels like a time machine. A tether.

After my dad passed away, Bobby and I met up with one of his best friends, Larry - his old business partner and one of the kindest men I know. A few weeks before, I had joked with my dad on the phone, "You should ask Larry to be my godfather."

We laughed.

But my dad called me back.

"I've got someone here who wants to tell you something."

"Hey Bethy," Larry said, with that same warmth he's always had.

"I'd be honored to be your godfather."

We all laughed. My dad was beaming. He loved a dramatic moment.

When we met Larry for lunch that day, I felt the comfort and the ache. Comfort because he has a way of making you feel like everything's going to be okay. And ache because every time I see him, I see my dad.

I couldn't help but tell him.

"I hope we can still see each other. Because when I'm around you, I feel like he's here."

We held hands, crying across the table. And then, I heard it.

One of my favorite Doobie Brothers songs playing in the restaurant.

I've never believed anything more than I did in that moment:

My dad was with us. And he wanted to make sure I knew it.

If my dad had it his way, I'm sure the Doobie Brothers would play every time I walk into a room. I like to think it's his version of saying, "I'm still here, Bumps."

And in those small moments, it feels like he never really left.

## 9 / THE WEIGHT OF IT ALL

I'm laying in the back of a Ford Expedition after my best friend's birthday party.

We were in third grade. She was a gymnast - petite, blonde, basically everything I wanted to be. I was taller than the other girls. Chubby. Frizzy brown hair.

Her party was at a farm, and my favorite part was riding the horses. I don't remember why I was in the back of the car - I just remember they thought I couldn't hear them.

But I could.

They were talking about me. About my weight. About how surprised they were that the horses could hold me.

I curled up on the floor and cried quietly, hoping they wouldn't realize I could hear them.

And that's when it started. I began training myself to be smaller in every way. To stay quiet. To blend in. To disappear.

I thought that maybe - if I could just fit in - they wouldn't make fun of me anymore. Back then, I really thought that was the goal - blend in, don't rock the boat, make yourself smaller so nobody notices the messy parts.

But it turns out, fitting in is overrated. And weirdly enough, it was a dog who taught me that.

Because if you get a dog who's even slightly spicy, dramatic, or emotionally complicated - it's not just a dog anymore. It's a mirror - reflecting your triggers, your childhood wounds, your control issues - basically all the stuff you'd rather not deal with but now have to... probably while walking your dog and probably in public. It's like the most unexpected personal-growth journey you'll ever go on.

Dogs like this ask you to lead when you feel lost. To set boundaries when you'd rather avoid. To stay calm when everything in you wants to react. To let go of the idea that you have to be perfect to be loved.

It's the transformation no one warns you about. But it's probably the one you needed the most.

# Part Two: The Messy Middle

## 10 / ROOTS FIRST

Two DAYS after I bought it, my rose bush looked like it was was one breeze away from becoming compost.

Drooping, dry at the edges, and clearly regretting its new home.

I stood there on the porch, hose in hand, staring at it like maybe sheer willpower could perk it back up.

I'd followed every tip the internet gave me - water in the morning, good drainage, plenty of light - and still, it looked miserable.

The guy at the nursery had warned me that roses were finicky, but I bought it anyway.

Honestly, I think I wanted to prove something.

Not to him - to the two high school girls I overheard at the farmer's market a few days earlier.

I was picking out herbs when they walked by, and one said, *"I can't wait until I'm an older woman and I can go shop-*

*ping for my garden."*

Older, not old.

Which, honestly, might be the best accidental compliment I've ever received.

So yeah, I walked into that nursery feeling like the cool older garden lady.

And I walked out with a rose bush.

Now here I was, forty-eight hours later, Googling "how to save a dying rose" like it was a medical emergency.

What if I ruined it?

Maybe I'm just bad at this?

What if I'm literally the only person who can kill a rose bush in two days?

I crouched down and touched one of the leaves - still soft, even if it looked defeated.

Maybe it wasn't about what it looked like right now.

Maybe it was about what it was trying to do.

And instantly, I thought about you.

About us and this whole dog ownership thing.

Because raising a dog - especially one who challenges you - can feel exactly like this.

It's messy at the beginning.

(Or, let's be honest, seven years in. Who's counting.)

It's full of doubts and chaos.

And sometimes, even when you're doing everything right, it still feels like nothing's happening.

So if you're in that "why isn't this working faster" season - if your dog still struggles and you feel like you're making a thousand mistakes - that doesn't mean you're bad at this.

And it doesn't mean everything you're doing is wrong.

It just means you're still underground, growing the stuff that matters most.

Roots first.

Bloom later.

## 11 / DIET PILLS

I'm standing in front of the mirror, pulling at the waistband of my leggings.

I'm not looking at myself, exactly - I'm scanning.

Flaws. Wrinkles. Pudge. Places I wish looked different.

Flatter stomach. Smoother skin. Just... less of me.

It's like my brain has a built-in software that auto-scans for imperfection.

I've had it for years.

If I'm thinner, I'll be more likable.

If I'm smaller, I'll take up less space.

And if I take up less space, I won't be judged, rejected or hurt.

I know how ridiculous it sounds when I say it out loud.

But when something gets wired into you at such a young age, it doesn't just go away because you *know better*.

In my senior year of high school, I started taking diet pills.

At first, it was just one bottle. Then two. Then I lost count.

I kept the empties hidden in the back of my closet, tucked into trash bags so my parents wouldn't see.

One day, I looked up and realized there were four full bags.

*I have to get rid of these. I can't get caught.*

That was my first thought.

Not *Is this dangerous?*

Or *why am I doing this?*

Just *Don't get caught.*

That's how deep it ran - the obsession with being smaller.

The thinner I got, the more praise I received.

And when the attention started coming, it felt like a drug.

Especially from guys.

It didn't matter if I liked them or not - what mattered was that they noticed me.

That someone finally looked at me and saw something worth wanting.


During the day, I skipped meals and popped pills.

At night, I lay awake for hours - my heart racing and brain buzzing.

But I told myself it was worth it.

That being thin was better than being tired.

That attention was better than hunger.

And then, out of nowhere, the pills stopped working. And my hunger came back stronger than ever.

And soon, the weight followed.

So did the shame.

I started skipping school because I didn't want anyone to see me.

I felt like I had failed at the one thing that finally made me *enough*.

I'd been thin. And now I wasn't.

What would people think?

I went from the girl who loved school - who talked to everyone -

to a kid hiding in her room and avoiding mirrors like they were punishment.

I missed so many days that I couldn't graduate with my class.

All my friends walked across the stage without me.


Later, I enrolled in night classes to finish my diploma.

And I did.

But I never really stopped feeling like a failure.

Like I'd messed up everything.

I didn't know it at the time, but I was learning how fragile a sense of worth can be when it's tied to what other people think of you.

And then I became a dog trainer - a job where it's *ridiculously* easy to measure yourself against the outcome. Where "good" means the dog listens perfectly, the owners are happy, and everyone thinks you're a dog whisperer.

So I started tying my worth to the progress I made with the dogs in front of me. If they struggled, I struggled. If they didn't turn out perfect, I didn't feel perfect either.

It was the same old shame in a new outfit.

Look at me. Too loud. Too messy. Too much. And maybe you've had your own version of that soundtrack on repeat.

But here's the thing: owning a challenging dog has a way of helping you rewrite that script. Because while you're busy training your dog, you're really training yourself too. You're learning not to disappear. Not to quiet yourself just to keep everyone else happy. You're figuring out a new way to measure worth that has nothing to do with perfection - and everything to do with showing up. It happens in the little moments: when you tell a stranger "no, he can't say hi" even though you hate the look they give you. When you keep walking past the neighbor's judgment instead of hiding inside on garbage day. When you hold the leash steady through your dog's meltdown instead of letting the shame pull you under. Those are the moments that count. That's you showing up.

So if you've ever felt like you had to take up less space to be accepted, let me remind you: you already belong. Exactly as you are. Your dog doesn't need some flawless version of you. They just need *you*. And that's more than enough.

## 12 / HAWKS

AND THERE IT WAS. Perched on the stop sign - and I just knew. It was him.

In dog training, I've learned to notice the small things most people overlook - the way a nervous dog's eyes soften for just a second, or the quiet sigh they let out when they finally settle. You learn to pay attention and trust that the quiet stuff can change everything. That's how it felt when I started noticing hawks everywhere - like they were letting me know I wasn't alone.

After a long few days at the hospital, I brought my mom home to shower and gather some things. While she got ready, I slipped into my dad's office - a space that always felt like him. I started pulling books from the shelves, flipping through the ones he read most often. Some had little scribbles in the margins, notes in his handwriting that made it feel like he was still sitting across from me at one of our usual coffee dates.

Tucked inside one of the books was a manila folder. Written at the top: facts about hawks.

I laughed. Or maybe just smiled - which, at the time, felt like a miracle.

I could picture him hearing a quote about hawks and instantly needing to know more. That was him - curious, thoughtful, always looking for meaning in things. He wasn't exactly tech-savvy, so the thought of him typing "hawk facts" into Google and carefully jotting things down in a folder was just ... so him.

In his writing: "Hawks never buy anything. They don't compare their nests. They claw and fight for survival. A lot to learn from the majestic hawk."

And then, of course - the stats:

"Red-tailed hawk - wingspan 52 inches. 4 to 5 feet from tip to tip."

I smiled and then just as quickly remembered I couldn't call or text him like I always did.

His notes made me miss him more - but also remember why I loved him so much. The mix was exhausting.


The next morning, a friend texted me a message that would carry me through some of the darkest times:

"Think of a sign. Something that feels like you two. When you see it, you'll know - he's still with you."

And instantly, I knew. A hawk.

How could it be anything else?

. . .

That afternoon, Bobby and I went for a drive - something we did all the time on weekends when we needed a reset. Driving through our favorite neighborhoods, windows down, lake views gliding by - it's our version of an escape. And that day, I needed it more than ever.

On our drive back to the hospital, we pulled up to a four-way stop.

I looked to my right and a giant hawk swooped down - landing on the stop sign just feet from my window.

My whole body went quiet. And I knew – it's my dad.


A few weeks later, I was getting my hair done and it was one of those "everything sucks" days. There's a big window by the hair-washing station, and it looks out onto this beautiful old oak tree. I laid there with my eyes closed, quietly whispering, please send me a hawk. Please, Dad. Let me know you're still here.

Minutes later my brother texted me.

"Look what showed up in our backyard! This never happens."

Attached was a video of a hawk, perched right in the middle of their yard.

I almost fell out of the chair, because – *are you kidding me?*

If there was ever a sign with his name written all over it - that was it. He always knew how to make an entrance.

And from that day on, I started looking for hawks. Not because I needed proof - but because I needed peace.

## 13 / TELL ME THE TRUTH

*"I'm struggling with infertility, and I just want to know - are kids really that great?" - me*

When you're in it - brand new to dog ownership or deep in a behavior you weren't prepared for - it can feel like you're the only one struggling. Like maybe you did something wrong and everyone else got the "easy dog" handbook.

That's how I felt when I couldn't get pregnant.

I thought having a baby was just what came next - like it was already written into the script of my life.

So when Bobby and I started trying, I thought it would happen easily. Instead, month after month, I rode the roller coaster of hope and disappointment, quietly questioning my womanhood. I never heard anyone talk about this kind of thing, and for a long time, I thought I was the only one going through it.

And of course, every time I opened Facebook it was just happy family photos and cute babies, like some kind of targeted ad for my insecurities. So, one day, I said 'screw it' and mid dog-walk posted on Facebook.

*"I'm struggling with infertility, and I just want to know - are kids really that great? Can someone tell me the not-so-cute stuff?"*

Looking back, it was a pretty bold move for 2012 me. But people responded. And not with judgment - with *relief.*

It was like I gave parents' permission to be real. They messaged me privately. They thanked me. They told me things they didn't feel comfortable saying out loud. That parenting isn't always magical. That some days, it's just keeping everyone alive and not losing your mind.

One person called me. An owner whose dog I walked every week - always bubbly, and the kind of person you instantly wanted to be friends with. She said my post made her feel seen. That she'd been struggling too. We ended up meeting for coffee the next day and talked for hours.

That conversation stuck with me - because being honest about my hard thing made space for someone else to share hers.

What I learned that day is that honesty doesn't push people away - it pulls them closer. And maybe that's the thing that makes all of this bearable: knowing we don't have to carry the hard parts alone.

Your dog's behavior isn't a reflection of your failure - it's an invitation for growth.

## 14 / DOGS AND SHAME

It happened at the vet.

Louie - our nervous German Shepherd - was shaking, and flailing around. I made the mistake of letting the techs take her to the back without me, something I now know I can - and should - insist on.

By the time they brought her back, there was blood on her paws. The tech holding her looked like she'd just ran a marathon.

And me?

I wanted to disappear.

My face flushed - heart pounding. And then the tech - clearly annoyed - delivered the line that stuck:

"Next time you bring her in, she needs to be on medication."

I nodded and smiled politely. But inside, I was mortified. I already felt like I was getting it all wrong with Louie and then this comment just proved I was right.

That day stayed with me. We found a new vet and moved on -

but I carried the embarrassment long after it was over.

Mostly because the harshest judgment wasn't coming from anyone else.

It was coming from me. That's the thing about feeling insecure about your dog - you start seeing signs everywhere that confirm it. Every side-eye from a stranger. Every bark. Every bad walk. Suddenly the mailman's avoiding eye contact and you're like, yep, even *he* knows I'm failing. And deep down, you're already halfway convinced you're not cut out for this.

I started noticing how tense I felt anytime Louie barked or rushed through a doorway. When friends came over - especially other trainers - I found myself always on edge, worried they'd walk away thinking, "She doesn't know what she's doing."

It wasn't until a friend of mine visited (who is also a trainer) and reminded me, "Hey, I've been there too," that something started to soften.

She didn't judge me or think less of Louie.

She reminded me that every dog comes with quirks.

And sometimes, that's all you need - reassurance that it's not just you.

One day, at our back door, everything changed.

I know, I know - dramatic much? But it kind of was.

Louie saw a squirrel, and like always, wanted to sprint outside and chase it up the fence.

Usually, I would've asked her to wait.

To be calm. To look like the well-trained dog I wanted the world to see.

You know - for our audience of zero in the kitchen.

But that day, I just opened the door and let her go.

She bolted outside – fast and happy.

And for once, I didn't try to stop her.

I just let her run.

I realized I'd been so focused on controlling how well trained she looked to others that I forgot to see her for who she actually was.

Training still matters. And boundaries, too.

But some things don't need fixing.

Some things just need room to breathe.

Louie isn't the dog I imagined I'd have.

But she's the dog I have.

And when I stopped comparing her to other dogs and trying to prove how good of a trainer I was through her, everything about our relationship felt easier.

Not overnight. But in the ways that mattered. Just between us.

You can't force someone - or a dog - to be who you want them to be.

But you *can* help bring out the best in who they actually are.

And yeah, that might look messier than it would with the chill dog down the street - but that's how it is for a lot of us. It doesn't mean you're doing it wrong. It just means your game plan might look a little different. You can choose the boundaries that matter and let go of the ones that don't. You can stop holding yourself to impossible standards built on someone else's highlight reel.

That's where things get a little easier.

Not perfect. Just... better. And sometimes "better" is what changes everything.

If you feel embarrassed by your dog's behavior - it's not just about them. It's about how hard you've tried to never be "too much" for anyone.

## 15 / TAKING UP SPACE

I'M STANDING in the hallway, waiting for my meds.

My parents dropped me off earlier that day, and now I'm here - alone, early twenties, in a treatment center full of strangers. The hallway smells like cleaning supplies and cafeteria food. Somewhere down the hall, someone's crying. Behind me, there's a bulletin board with inspirational quotes pinned up with thumbtacks. I read the same one three times just to keep my eyes busy.

In some ways, it felt like déjà vu - the hallways, the smell of disinfectant, the sense of being both surrounded and completely alone. Like the psych ward, just minus the man whose idea of small talk was asking to suck on my toes. This place came with its own kind of discomfort.

I'm at Renfrew, an eating disorder treatment center for women. I spent years in cycles of bingeing, shame, restriction, repeat. The kind of stuff you hide behind "I'm just not hungry" or "I already ate earlier." I used the label *bulimia* when I talked about it - because that's the one people seemed to take seriously. Because somewhere along the way, even the labels felt like they had a hierarchy. And I still wanted to be the *right kind* of broken.

I didn't feel like I fit in. I wasn't "sick enough." I hadn't lost enough weight. I didn't have the kind of body that people imagine when they hear "eating disorder." But I was unraveling inside. Food was my control and my punishment. My escape and my enemy. I hated how much space I took up. Literally.

And then I met Josie.

She was 13 - blonde, tiny, a gymnast with bright blue eyes. She reminded me so much of my childhood best friend it was almost eerie. Josie had the kind of smallness that made people want to protect her. I remember thinking: *If I looked like her, would I be taken more seriously?*

During my second week, we started going on group outings. A supervised trip to Target. The goal, according to our therapist, was *exposure.* Try on clothes. Notice what it brought up. Therapy in the fitting room. Sounds fun, right?

Somehow, I got grouped with the Renfrew rebels - girls who were bold and blunt and very much over it. One of them had refused her meds that morning. Another ran away later that week. I didn't talk much. I just followed them around like a weird little intern. They terrified me - but I also wanted to be like them. They didn't seem to care what people thought. Or maybe they cared, but were too exhausted to hide it anymore.

At Target, one of them held up a pair of bright green parachute pants. They looked like someone had sewn two sleeping bags together and called it fashion.

"These," she said. "These are the pants. We're all getting them. Fuck jeans."

I laughed, assuming she wasn't serious.

She lit a cigarette as we left the store and shouted over her shoulder, "None of us want to put on jeans right now. Fuck the size of your jeans and how it makes you feel. You're more than a number. Just wear the pants and give yourself a break."

And maybe it was the rebellion. Or the weird solidarity of that cigarette pep talk. Or the fact that I had been feeling so bloated and ashamed that even my sweatpants felt aggressive. But I bought the pants.

A few pairs, actually.

They were ridiculous - billowy and loud and *definitely not slimming*. But when I put them on, something in me exhaled. I didn't feel beautiful. But I felt...free-er. And in that moment, free felt more important than beautiful.

Not to be dramatic, but those pants changed me. Because underneath all the shame, all the fear and image management and wanting to be the *right kind of girl* - I just wanted to feel *okay*.

I wanted to feel like I belonged in my body. To take up space without apologizing. To stop holding my breath waiting for someone to say I was enough.

I didn't know it at the time, but those pants were my first act of rebellion against the version of myself I thought I *had* to be - small, polished, easy to understand.

Fast forward a few years, and I found myself in a different kind of spiral. Only this time, I wasn't in a treatment center. I was on a sidewalk, holding the leash of a dog who was barking her head off at a skateboard.

People were staring.

My face was flushed.

And all I could think was: *What do they think of me?*

I wasn't just embarrassed.

I was exposed.

Because this wasn't the image I had in my head.

I wanted to be the calm, confident dog trainer. The one who knew exactly what to do. The one with the well-behaved dog who ignored distractions and made people say, "Wow, she's such a good trainer."

Instead, I got a dog who made me feel like I was right back in that Renfrew hallway - nervous and feeling like too much.

And just like before, the shame didn't come from the behavior itself. It came from what I *thought* the behavior said about me.

That I didn't belong.

And I was the only one struggling this much.

I thought I had outgrown that version of myself - the one who obsessed over how she looked and who people wanted her to be.

But then I worked with a dog who didn't care about my image.

She cared about how she felt.

And that meant I had to stop performing and actually *show up* to help her through it.

Not as the perfect trainer.

But as someone willing to be seen.

Someone who showed up anyway - messy, unsure, and still trying.

Each walk felt like an act of courage.

And by courage, I mean putting on real pants and stepping outside even though I was already mentally rehearsing what I'd say if someone gave us a dirty look.

But still - I went.

Even when it was uncomfortable and I felt like everyone was watching.

Because every walk like that quietly chipped away at my need to be liked, understood, or approved of.

And underneath all of that?

Something sturdier started to grow.

Not tougher necessarily. Just… steadier.

Like I could finally take up space without apologizing for it.

Because dogs like this shape you into someone who cares less about how things *look* and more about what's actually *true*.

## 16 / LESS SHRINKING, MORE SPEAKING UP

ONCE YOU START SPEAKING up for your dog, you realize just how much you tiptoe in other areas of your life.

Like the amount of time I've spent wondering if too many exclamation points would make me seem obnoxious (God forbid I annoy someone with my zest for life) or if too few emojis would make someone think I was mad at them? Embarrassing.

(And listen - if I ever respond to your text with just "Thanks." instead of a cheerful "Thank you! *heart emoji*" - you should probably call a therapist. Because something has gone awry.)

We overthink *everything.*

So of course we overthink what people think of us when we set boundaries with our dogs. Especially when someone acts like they're the exception. Or when your dog suddenly starts barking and lunging at the neighbor in the hat - the same neighbor they've seen every single day of their life.

It's not just the moment itself. It's the mental replay afterward, wondering what that person now thinks about you.

Back in my early twenties, I worked the front desk at a golf shop in the local country club.

And there was one golf pro who was...

(insert every red flag emoji ever)

He was funny.

He was charming.

He was wildly inappropriate when no one else was around.

At the time, I was young and struggling with my confidence.

So when he made crude jokes or flirted, part of me felt flattered.

(UGH. It hurts to even type that.)

Most of the time, I'd laugh along - even when I felt like I needed a shower afterward.

Until one day, I set the tiniest boundary:

I didn't laugh at one of his jokes.

Easy enough, right?

Wrong.

He poked my stomach - like physically poked me - and made a comment about my weight.

I said, as calmly as I could,

"Hey. Please don't do that."

And he... did it again.

I remember trying to sound "nice" when I set the boundary.

I remember working so hard not to seem "too sensitive."

(A label I'd been handed more times than I could count.)

And when he threw his hands up and said,

"Whoa, whoa! I was just messing with you!"

I felt...

shame.

Embarrassment.

Like somehow I was the problem for saying anything at all.

And that moment?

It taught me something that's taken years to unlearn:

Setting a boundary doesn't make you wrong.

It doesn't make you sensitive.

And it definitely doesn't make you rude.

It makes you strong.

Even if your hands are shaking.

Even if you cry in the car afterward.

So if you read that story and felt a little protective of me -

I want you to channel that energy when someone ignores your "Don't pet my dog" boundary.

Because if you felt even a flicker of anger on my behalf?

That's exactly how I feel about people disrespecting yours.

Saying, "Please don't pet my dog," might seem like nothing. But if you've ever swallowed your discomfort to keep someone else happy, you know it's actually kind of huge.

It's the moment you decide you're not here to make random strangers comfortable at the expense of yourself - or your dog. It's you ditching the fake smile, skipping the awkward laugh, and just saying the thing.

And yeah, maybe your hands sweat. Maybe you replay the whole thing later and think, *Ugh, did I sound mean?* But here's the thing - you did it anyway.

So the next time someone ignores your boundary? I hope you remember that you've already practiced standing up for both of you. And I hope you give yourself the same protective energy you'd give me if you saw some old golf pro poking me in the stomach.

Because that? That's the real win.

You don't have to be the most confident owner or the most put-together human to deserve good things. You just have to keep showing up - messy, nervous, hopeful, all of it. That's enough.

## 17 / COMFORT ZONES

*"You have two choices. You can let this break you. Or you can flip it - and change how the story ends." - Joe Mangascle*

It was my first year of training, and most of the dogs I worked with were pushy but manageable - boxers who jumped too much, doodles who dragged their owners down the sidewalk like a team of sled dogs. Nothing that made me nervous.

And then there was George.

I met his owners in a parking lot.

He was sweet, a little reserved. She smiled like sunshine, hugged me immediately and I liked them instantly. The kind of people you want to help, even if you're not totally sure you can.

Their dream was to travel the country in an RV with their dog.

Which, fun fact, was the same exact dream I was writing about in my journal every morning. So yeah - this felt personal. Like the universe assigned me a couple who would 100% be my best friends in another life.

George, unfortunately, didn't feel like a sign. He felt like a challenge I maybe wasn't ready for.

Separation anxiety.

Reactivity.

A prey drive so high he once launched himself out the front door after a neighbor's dog.

We sat at a picnic table behind the airstream they were renovating. They told me how much they loved George. How hard they were trying.

And I could feel it - that quiet shame of loving a dog who makes life harder.

Or wondering if people are judging you.

And wondering if maybe they're right.

I took a breath and said, *"I've never worked with a case like this before... but I'd really love to help you."*

Without hesitation they said, *"Great! That's all we need."*

And that was the moment I learned something big:

Most owners aren't asking for perfect.

They just need to know there's still hope.

. . .

About two weeks into his board and train, I hit a full emotional wall. Picture me lying on the couch with a diffuser and lavender oil basically shooting up my nose, trying to calm down while George whined from his kennel like we were both being held hostage.

If you've ever lived with a dog like him - anxious, reactive, easily worked up - you know what I mean. You're not just managing their emotions. You're absorbing them and that's usually when you start second-guessing everything.

What you're doing.

What they need.

Whether you're even qualified to be in charge of another living thing.

It's exhausting.

And weirdly personal.

Like, how did this 65-pound tornado unlock all my unresolved self-worth issues?

I started asking the big dramatic questions:

• Why did I say yes to working with this dog?

• I thought being a dog trainer was supposed to be fun.

• Why does no one talk about the parts that make you want to scream into a pillow and move to the woods?

Eventually I did the one thing I'm historically bad at:

I asked for help.

I reached out to a trainer friend with more experience and fully braced myself for judgment or a "maybe this career isn't for you" pep talk. Instead, she was kind. Supportive. Zero ego.

And it clicked.

When something - or someone - is struggling, there's no room for ego. There's just the next right step. If you have a dog like George, you're probably already braver than you think.

Because you're doing the hardest things without even realizing it:

• Showing up when you're exhausted.

• Learning while completely overwhelmed.

• Loving your dog through all the doubt.

It might not look the way you thought it would.

It might feel slower and messier.

But that doesn't mean it isn't working.

Growth, especially with dogs, rarely feels good in the moment.

It's not clean and it's not cute. But it's worth it to to try.

When I think back on George, it's not the messy stuff I remember most. It's the glimmers. The first time he walked past another dog without losing it. The first time his owners sent me a selfie of the three of them having a picnic at a busy park.

Those moments were small. But they were everything.

And when I wanted to give up, when it felt like I was failing at something I really cared about, I thought about what my dad used to tell me:

*"You have two choices.*

*You can let this break you.*

*Or you can flip it - and change how the story ends."*

That's the magic.

Not being perfect.

Not getting it right the first time.

But flipping the hard parts into something you're proud of.

Even if you're diffusing lavender into your face like it's your new personality.

You're doing it.

You're still here.

And that matters more than you know.

## 18 / SOFTNESS IS A STRENGTH

Do I need to be more stern? More alpha with my dog? I worry that I'm too soft.

In my second year as a dog trainer, I was deep in comparison mode - constantly watching what other trainers were doing and, in a weird way, using their confidence to validate my own insecurities.

As much as I hated feeling that way, sometimes it's almost easier to believe you're not good enough.

Around that time, I started talking with an older male trainer out in California. He was a friend of the trainer who led a seminar I attended the year before, and at first, he seemed encouraging. He commented on my social media posts, told me how proud he was of how far I'd come since the workshop.

When your confidence is shaky, that kind of feedback feels like a lifeline.

And then one day, it changed.

He started telling me I needed to toughen up.

That being a sensitive trainer wouldn't get me far.

That if I really wanted to help owners and their dogs, I'd need to be more assertive.

More alpha.

More... like him.


But something about the way he spoke to me made me shrink.

Like I was a little girl again, nodding along to a big brother who knew better. And for a while, I believed him.


A week later, he messaged me an offer to come out and shadow him.

"It'll be good for your confidence," he said.

"Help toughen you up a little."

I brought the idea to Bobby.

"Umm - what? No. You don't need to toughen up. Who is this guy?"

And seriously - what was I thinking?

Sometimes I worry my risk of being lured into a cult is... high. Or maybe my confidence was just so low, I couldn't see how bad of an idea it really was.

But I try to have compassion for that version of myself.

The one who didn't know you could be soft and strong at the same time.

I used to think I had to change who I was to be a great trainer - mostly because I didn't see many examples of trainers who were softer.

And how do you know it's okay to be different when all you've seen is one way?

It's the same for you with your dog.

None of us brought a dog home thinking, I can't wait for this to feel overwhelming and make me question everything about myself. That'll be fun!

It's normal to feel like you're not good enough when you're first figuring out life with a challenging dog.

Especially once you start researching training methods or following new accounts online - your judgment gets cloudy. Your gut instinct gets muddled.

How are you supposed to trust yourself when you've never done this before?

I've worked with so many owners who worry that their softness is the problem. That their dog won't take them seriously unless they're more "alpha." But what I've found is that softness, when paired with structure, is a strength.

If you're a softer owner and you let everything slide, you might struggle. But if you're someone who speaks softer, avoids yelling, and wants to build trust - leaning into structure throughout your dog's day is exactly how you protect that kindness from being taken advantage of.

And the funny thing? The dogs who need the most structure usually end up with the people who need a reason to find their voice. The ones who've spent years softening their edges, avoiding conflict, keeping the peace. And if you're reading this thinking, "yep, that's me - I feel too soft for my dog," maybe that's the point. Maybe you got this dog because life knew you were ready to step into the kind of leader your dog (and you) have been waiting for.

## 19 / SWEATY PITS

I was wearing a bright pink blouse at a middle school dance.

And it should be said: I was a sweaty kid. My armpits almost always showed up at the very first sign of nerves. It's like they could sense my teenage awkwardness and thought, nope. We refuse to let you look cute today - especially at a time in your life when all you want is to fit in. Instead, we're going to treat you like a sweaty old man who starts perspiring the second he even *thinks* about sweating.

My pits always showed themselves. And in my flamingo-pink blouse, I felt like you could see the sweat stains from space.

Talking about it makes me feel like I'm right back in middle school - under those awful gym lights, lined up for something humiliating like the rope climb in PE. The teacher calls my name, thirty kids are watching, and I make it maybe two feet before sliding back down. I laugh it off, but really I just want the floor to swallow me whole.

We all have our rope climb moment. And here's the thing - walking a dog who's louder, more reactive, or just more than the others in your neighborhood? It's the same exact feeling. That rush of insecurity, like everyone's watching and judging, even if they're not.

And suddenly, you're not just walking your dog. You're back in middle school, praying no one notices you and hoping to disappear into the wall before anyone sees how hard you're trying. Because it's not just about the barking or the lunging or the sweating through your blouse. It's about the quiet panic of being found out.

Like your dog is giving away the secret - that you're not the effortlessly calm, put-together owner you wish you were.

You're just some damp, anxious mess trying to survive the walk.

But here's what I didn't realize then - and what I've only started to understand now, thanks to getting dogs who don't exactly fit in:

You don't have to be effortless to be worthy. You can sweat through your shirt, get tangled in the leash, say the wrong thing when walking past your neighbor as your dog almost pulls you over - and still be the exact person your dog needs.

And sometimes, the dog who makes it harder to disappear is the one who finally teaches you not to.

If you've spent years trying not to upset
anyone, trying to be the 'good girl' -
then having a dog who doesn't follow
the rules might be the first time
you start rewriting your own.

## 20 / BOUNDARIES

I'M STANDING in Home Depot with a training dog named Nellie. She's white, with black and tan spots all over - an excitable young dog, around seven months old.

A man stops us.

"Can I pet her? She's so cute!"

He's nice, and I feel bad - but I'm trying to get Nellie to calm down in places like this and ignore people. She's known to get overly excited when anyone pays attention to her. And lately, I've been pushing myself to speak up more - to set boundaries, even when it feels uncomfortable. This felt like one of those moments.

"No, she's in training. But thanks for asking."

His tone shifts.

"You know," he says, "you shouldn't bring a dog somewhere like this if you won't let people pet her."

And then he walks off.

Um - what just happened?

I was a new dog trainer and this old cranky man left me feeling like I'd done something wrong. My lifetime of people-pleasing did not prepare me for this.

But here's what I know now: every time you set a boundary - even if your voice shakes or someone gives you a look - you get a little more comfortable holding your ground.

And that's been the surprising part of working with dogs like Nellie. They've forced me to face the parts of myself I spent years avoiding - especially my need to be liked.

For so long, I bent over backwards to make people happy. I said what they wanted to hear. I became who they expected. I stayed small, quiet, full protection mode. But dogs? They didn't need me to be likable. They needed me to lead.

And surprisingly, the thing that helped me the most was learning to set boundaries for them.

One of the best examples of that? The phrase: *"No, you can't pet my dog."*

It seems simple. But if "people-pleaser" sits at the top of your personality résumé, it's not simple. When I first started working with dogs who needed me to say no to hello's, I had to give myself a full-on pep talk before going anywhere. It felt exactly like prepping for an awkward conversation with a friend or family member - the kind where you rehearse it twenty different ways just in case it goes badly.

Because anytime you have to do something outside the "just smile and keep everyone happy" zone? Hello, sweaty pits.

Nothing makes you feel worse than telling a kid they can't pet your dog. It's basically the emotional equivalent of telling them Santa isn't real. Some people look at you like you've personally ruined their day. And you must hate joy. Obviously.

But the more I did it, the more I realized I wasn't just teaching a dog to be calm in public. I was learning how to take up space myself. Owning a challenging dog comes with a side effect no one warns you about - you start setting boundaries for them, and suddenly, you start setting them for yourself, too.

And honestly? Once you get a taste of that confidence, it's kind of addictive - in the best way. You start wondering where else in your life you've been playing small... and what might happen if you stopped.

I didn't get the dog who blended in.
I got the dog who made me feel like
an outsider - until I learned how to
stand up for the both of us.

Part Three: Just when you think you've got it all figured out ...

Some dogs challenge you.

Some dogs heal you.

And some dogs do both.

## 21 / IT'S FEEDBACK, NOT A SETBACK

THE TRUTH ABOUT REACTIVITY? It's messy. One minute you're feeling proud, the next you're googling, "do other people's dogs act like this??" One day you're basically a certified dog training queen - like maybe you should start charging strangers in the park for your wisdom. And then Wednesday rolls around and your dog is acting like they've never heard a single word you've ever said.

Dog training amnesia.

Love that for us.

When I was working with Susie - a small, black terrier-mix with a few white spots and a lot of opinions - I lived this on repeat.

Susie was sweet and also very loud.

Not just bark-loud.

More like fire-alarm-in-a-hallway loud.

She was one of the most reactive dogs I'd worked with, and even though we were making great progress by the end of her training, outings were still... a lot.

One day after a walk, she had a full meltdown getting back into the car as another dog walked by.

And not the cute kind - like, "oh, Susie's just being silly."

But the kind that makes every person in the parking lot stop and stare.

I managed to get her settled, got into the car myself ... and immediately started crying.

Maybe it was my luteal phase.

Or maybe it was the fact that I was deep in my "compare yourself to every trainer on Instagram" era.

And in that moment, every embarrassing second felt like proof I wasn't good enough.

Proof that no matter how hard I tried, I was still failing.

Because no one talks about the part where you're doing everything right - and still feel like you're screwing it all up.

That's when I came up with a little mantra I still use today:

It's feedback, not a setback.

And I said it over and over again.

Because here's the truth:

One messy moment doesn't erase your progress.

It doesn't mean you're back at square one.

It just means you're learning - both of you.

Now, every time I hit a rough moment - whether with a dog, myself, or life in general - I try to get curious instead of judgmental.

Not: I'm the worst trainer to ever exist.

But: What happened right before that?

- Could I have tightened up our walking rules?
- Did I miss a chance to advocate for her sooner?
- What can I prep differently next time?

Because honestly?

It's not that different from the rest of life:

You finally start feeling grounded ... and one weird conversation throws you off.

You eat clean all week, and then spiral over chips and queso.

You promise to set better boundaries ... and then say yes to something you absolutely did not want to do.

None of that means you failed.

It just means you're human.

So the next time your dog has a messy moment and you find yourself dramatically declaring that you're the worst?

Pause – breathe – and remember:

It's not a setback.

It's just feedback.

And you're doing better than you think.

I didn't get the calm, confident dog.

I got the one who mirrored my anxiety

and made me face it.

## 22 / JOHNNY

It's been seven years since we brought Theo home, and I'm in one of those familiar seasons - desperate for change.

But this time, it's not about purpose or direction.

I'm trying to outrun my grief.

My dad passed away eight months ago, and I still don't know how to live in a world without him.

I want something that feels like a reset.

Something to keep me from coming apart at the seams.

Part of me wants to pack a bag and hike the Appalachian Trail - one of those wild, life-altering things people do in memoirs when they've completely lost the plot and need to prove they can survive something.

But instead, we drive to the animal shelter on a Saturday to "look" at dogs.

(This is how we ended up with four dogs, by the way.)

I meet a few, but none of them feel like mine.

It's only when we're about to leave that I see him - smaller than I'd pictured, with a brindle coat flecked in dark brown and black.

A big, blocky head.

Cautious eyes that study before they move.

"He was dropped off this morning with two siblings," the volunteer says.

He's not the kind of dog I usually go for - but I crouch down and press my hand to the gate anyway.

He edges closer, slow like he's testing the ground.

One lick to my hand.

Then he's still again.

I wasn't sure if he was my dog - but I was curious enough to find out.

We're led into a small room with a bench and bright yellow walls plastered with flyers and volunteer notes. The door opens, and when he comes in, he immediately ducks under the bench to hide.

I lower myself onto the cold cement floor, a few feet away, and tap my leg.

Nothing.

I tap again.

He inches forward - slow, cautious - until he's close enough to sniff me.

I hold my palm up and he lays his head down in my hand like it's the most natural thing in the world.

He stays long enough to feel like something just shifted.

I didn't take him home that day. Not yet.

He needed a little more time at the shelter. And honestly, I needed a little more time before bringing him home. So I left with a deposit slip - proof he was officially on hold.

No one else could take him.

But it bought me a few days to make sure I wasn't just chasing an impulse.

The maybe-this-is-him feeling was buzzing in my chest, right next to: *What the hell am I doing?*

We already had four dogs.

Five felt... excessive.

What are we, insane?

The next morning, Bobby and I went for a walk to talk it through.

We found a bench by the lake and started our pro/con list - the routines, the other dogs, what life would look like with one more.

Midway through, a bird pooped on my shoulder.

I know - EW. But, also -

"Is this a sign?!" I asked, half-joking, half-not.

We'd spent the last year seeing hawks at the most meaningful moments.

Sure, I had a habit of reading too much into things, but this one?

Felt like a nudge.

A wink from my dad.

Or maybe just proof that signs don't have to be sparkly to be real.

Sometimes, it's just... poop.

On Sunday, we were in the pool, still undecided, when I heard it - the cry of a hawk.

I hadn't seen one in months, but that week they kept showing up.

Every day after meeting my new maybe-dog. And the more I noticed, the harder it became to ignore what was right in front of me.


Monday morning, I drove back to get him - hands shaky on the steering wheel, Johnny Cash blasting through the speakers like the music might either calm me down or seal the deal.

Part of me still wasn't sure.

The other part was hoping this dog might be the thing that kept me standing.

When we got home, I walked him around the backyard.

He sniffed everything like he was memorizing it.

And then I heard it - another hawk, perched in the tree across the street.

It was like someone wanted to make sure I knew.

That this dog was something special.

A dog whose birthday, I'd later learn, might be the same as my dad's: February 3rd.

In the weeks that followed, the hawks kept coming.

Every day.

Like my dad was making sure I didn't miss the message.

I didn't hike the Appalachian Trail.

I didn't survive months of blisters or carry my life on my back.

Instead, I walked into an animal shelter and came home with a nervous dog who, in his own way, would end up being just as much of a test - and maybe the thing that saved me.

Maybe it was coincidence.

Or maybe it was a quiet reminder that my dad is still with me - sending what I need, exactly when I need it.

Me with Johnny the first time I met him at the shelter.

## 23 / FIRST IMPRESSIONS AREN'T THE FULL STORY

THERE'S ALMOST ALWAYS a moment after you bring home a new dog when you want to hit the panic button.

The *what did we just do* button.

The *this wasn't in the brochure* button.

For me, it happened the first night we brought Johnny home. The dog I was sure would fix everything, because clearly that's how dogs work, right? But now, he was barking and crying in his kennel like we'd personally ruined his life.

Later that day, I sat on the couch with Bobby, sipping wine and trying to pretend I wasn't internally spiraling.

Johnny was barking from the other room - each bark making me seriously question all my life choices.

I looked at Bobby and said, "Did I just ruin everything?"

He stayed calm - like he always does - and said, "Let's just give it one more day. See if he settles a little better tomorrow."

This felt all too familiar.

Years earlier, I'd said almost the exact same thing to him about Theo - and now here we were again, crossing our fingers and hoping the next 24 hours wouldn't break us.

That night, I posted something vague on Instagram about my new dog and how things weren't going great. Someone replied and said, *"It sounds like the adoption blues. I went through that, too."*

I'd never heard that phrase before, but it made me feel so much better. Because the truth is - I didn't feel connected to Johnny yet.

I felt tired.

Overwhelmed.

Regretful, even.

And then I felt ashamed for feeling all of that.

And even though I'd felt this kind of regret years before with Theo, it didn't feel any easier with Johnny.

But this time, I knew enough to wait it out.

So in case you're there right now, here's what I want you to know:

**First impressions aren't the full story.**

What you're noticing - the whining, the pacing, the meltdown over the trash can - isn't who your dog *is*.

Maybe that's who they are when they're overstimulated and a little unsure of the world they just landed in.

But you're meeting your dog at their most uncertain.

The bonding might not feel instant, but that doesn't mean it's not happening.

It just means you're in the thick of a big transition - and big transitions are rarely easy.

So if you're sitting in the quiet chaos of new dog life, wondering if you've made a mistake - odds are, you haven't.

You're just in the part no one really talks about.

The part where everything feels a little unhinged, your dog might be possessed, and nothing feels settled yet - but also? It's not just you.

**Things I Wish Someone Told Me**

It's normal to feel regret. That doesn't mean you picked the wrong dog.

Bonding isn't always instant. Sometimes it's awkward, slow, and starts with side-eyes.

You can love your dog *and* feel completely overwhelmed by them.

Guilt is going to try to move in. Don't let it unpack.

Your dog's behavior isn't a reflection of your worth.

Google can be helpful - or it can ruin your whole night. Tread carefully.

You might miss your old routine. That doesn't make you selfish.

The moment things start to click probably won't feel dramatic - it'll feel quiet, and kind of boring. That's good.

If you're spiraling, go outside. Take a breath. Text someone who gets it.

And it's not just you. *Really*. It's not.

## 24 / THE WOLF

I DOVE headfirst into the van before my brain could catch up.

Because standing about twenty feet away from us

was a Yellowstone wolf.

Not a coyote.

Not a really big dog.

A wolf.

In February 2020, Bobby and I bought our dream camper van - something we'd been talking about for years.

We pictured it perfectly: traveling the country with our dogs, living our best National Geographic life, sipping coffee in scenic campsites, creating memories we'd talk about forever.

And honestly?

Most of that happened.

(Minus the part where I nearly had a heart attack in Yellowstone, but we'll get to that.)

Traveling with four big dogs isn't for everyone.

But for us, it just felt right.

Homebody energy? Cranked.

Anxious dogs who don't love new people? Handled.

Pet sitters who could manage our crew? Uh... not really a thing.

Bringing our "home" on the road was the obvious answer.

And the dogs thrived.

No boarding stress.

No awkward meet-and-greets.

Just our little pack, doing life together.

After a few practice trips - quick loops through Georgia and North Carolina - we planned the Big One:

Out West.

Grand Teton. Yellowstone. Bucket list stuff.

We were ready.

(Narrator: They were not ready.)

Grand Teton was everything we'd hoped for - breathtaking views, wide-open spaces, off-leash dogs frolicking against mountain backdrops like we were filming a Subaru commercial.

But Yellowstone?

Yellowstone had a surprise waiting for us.

It was still dark when we pulled over for a quick bathroom break.

Louie, our cautious German Shepherd, was first out of the van - off-leash, like usual.

She never strays far.

Bobby scanned the area with a flashlight.

First on Louie.

Then to the right.

And that's when we saw it.

A massive grey wolf.

Close enough to make eye contact.

Close enough that my knees stopped existing.

"WOLF! LOUIE, COME!"

I didn't think.

I dove into the van and Louie followed - like we'd been training for this moment her whole life.

We slammed the doors and watched from the window as the wolf strolled off, completely unfazed.

As if we were the ones out of place.

Which, honestly?

Fair.

I wish I could say I watched a Yellowstone wolf from a safe distance, coffee in hand, marveling at the beauty of nature.

But no. I blacked out, screamed like a maniac, and belly-flopped into the van. That trip - wolf and all - changed something in me as a dog owner. Because traveling with dogs doesn't just give you good stories. It teaches you things - and a big one is flexibility.

You plan for calm mornings and get chaos instead.

You plan for scenic hikes and end up sprinting back to the van.

It teaches you awareness.

Not just of your surroundings, but of your dogs - their limits, their stress signals, the tiny ways they're trying to tell you, "Hey, I'm not okay with this."

It teaches you advocacy.

You realize quickly that "my dog needs space" isn't just a cute bandana - it's a real responsibility.

And it's okay if that means skipping the crowded trail, the busy brewery, or the off-leash park where someone's dog has zero recall.

You learn that planning ahead doesn't make you uptight.

It makes the whole trip more enjoyable - for you and your dog.

You learn that sometimes, the biggest wins aren't Instagram-worthy moments.

They're the quiet ones - your dog curled up peacefully at your feet while the world moves outside your window.

. . .

I used to think traveling with dogs meant:

- Wide open spaces and off-leash freedom
- Perfect recall
- No stress, no drama, just golden-hour magic

But real life?

It's messy and imperfect.

It's getting up at 5 a.m. to avoid crowds.

Having a backup plan for your backup plan.

Or diving into the van while you pray this is the time your dog listens to you.

And weirdly?

That's where the real magic happens.

Because it's not about having a perfect adventure.

It's about doing life together -

wild, unexpected, and maybe a little dangerous.

From left to right: Sadie, Theo, Louie, and Charlie in the van on our Yellowstone trip.

I didn't get the dog I expected.

I got the dog who saved me in

ways I didn't see coming.

## 25 / EVEN WHEN YOUR DOG IS DOING BETTER, YOUR BODY MIGHT NOT BELIEVE IT

I TURNED my back for what felt like a second to sweep the porch. And that's when I heard it - the growling. The scramble of nails on concrete.

I turned around and saw our dog Sadie locked in a fight with Ginger, a dog I watched regularly.

I started screaming for help and tried to pull them apart. Every time I got one off, the other jumped back in. Neither one backing down.

I thought they'd kill each other.

Eventually, I managed to drag Sadie onto the porch and slam the door shut behind her. My body was shaking from the adrenaline. What just happened? Everything was fine two minutes ago.

The dogs were okay. But me? I didn't recover for a long time.

I was a pet sitter and dog walker. Fighting dogs were not on my radar.

A few months later, I stood outside an animal shelter.

I wanted to get into dog training, but part of me was convinced that my fear of dogs fighting meant I wasn't cut out for it. A friend suggested I volunteer - said it would give me more experience with dogs. Build my confidence.

It was summer in Florida, which meant I was already sweating through my volunteer shirt ten minutes in. My yellow name tag curled at the edges. My camera - heavy and awkward - swung against my hip.

I'd fallen in love with photography as a dog walker and loved sending pictures to owners. There's something about looking through a lens that changes how you see things.

At orientation, they touched on dog fights and what to do if one broke out.

"Bang two metal bowls together really loud," she said.

That's it?

I remember writing it down thinking: *This cannot be the full strategy*.

-

Volunteering didn't calm my nerves. If anything, it made them worse.

One day, I was in the play yard with another volunteer who suggested we bring out two dogs together for free time. I picked up a leash that felt more like a shoestring and walked over to Tom's kennel.

He was a 75-pound gray pitbull mix who'd been dropped off that morning. As I approached, he started jumping against the gate, and I froze.

That's when I realized - it's dogs like Tom that put me on edge. Not because of his breed. But because dogs like this have an energy that feels unpredictable. Like it could turn into something bad and that made me feel all kinds of anxious.

-

I can't get that vision out of my head.

Ginger foaming at the mouth, launching herself at Sadie. I'm screaming. Trying to break them apart.

The next day, I search for Dog Whisperer episodes and specifically look for ones about dogs who fight.

The one I find is about two dogs who live together. Cesar Millan brings them to his dog psychology center. Everything seems calm - until it's not. They fight. They latch on. I start sweating just watching it.

After what feels like forever, they finally break them apart. Cesar's out of breath. He tells the owners the dogs aren't a good match and offers to keep one, so they can both live happy lives - just not together.

-

I'm back at the shelter. Standing close to the gate so Tom doesn't sneak past me.

I'm already nervous about bringing him into the play yard with another dog.

What if they fight? What if we can't stop it? What then?

I have very little faith in the "bang bowls together" plan.

Later, I learned that breaking up dog fights isn't what makes someone a good trainer. Learning how to read dogs is.

Taking cues. Watching body language. Anticipating what happens next.

And over the next few years, the more dogs I worked with, the more confident I felt. It didn't happen overnight - or even in the first years of training. It was slow. A process of learning to trust myself, my instincts, and my way of doing things, even when it didn't look like what other trainers were doing.

I still struggled with my confidence into my fourth year as a dog trainer. I'd find myself hesitating anytime two dogs played in my backyard.

I wanted so badly to move on. To feel confident. But my body wouldn't let me forget.

That memory came rushing back recently when working with an owner whose confidence was at an all-time low.

Her dog had a long history of reactivity and he was with me for training.

During one of our text check-ins, she wrote:

"My confidence is so low. It's hard to be confident on walks when I keep thinking about how reactive he's been for the last three years."

And something clicked. Something I hadn't fully put into words before:

Even when your dog starts doing better on walks , your body might not believe it yet.

That's what I call Reactive Muscle Memory (RMM).

It's that tightening in your chest at the sight of another dog - even if yours is calmly sniffing the sidewalk. It's your nervous system acting like it's still 2020 and your dog is lunging and barking at the German shepherd who lives down the block.

It's like your body doesn't want to forget.

Just like me - years later - still feeling my heart race when supervising dogs playing. Even when everything is going great.

-

The hardest part about Reactive Muscle Memory is that no one tells you it's a thing.

No one warns you that your dog's progress doesn't automatically undo the panic your body has learned over the years.

And that doesn't mean you're failing. Or doing it wrong. It just means you're still healing.

The more you keep showing up - even if you're unsure or holding the leash a little tighter than you meant to - the more those patterns start to soften.

This isn't just about reactivity training. It's nervous system rehab.

You're not just helping your dog feel safe in the world.

You're helping yourself feel safe in it again, too.

## 26 / HATEFUL JEANS

I'M NEVER WEARING jeans again.

I have maybe six pieces of clothing I rotate throughout the week - mostly workout stuff, plus my favorite old yellow "house shorts" (please tell me I'm not the only one) and an oversized Nike shirt Bobby wore in high school.

The rest of my clothes are crammed into a dresser, and the jeans? Buried at the bottom.

I try my best not to wear them because - if we're being real - it's that stupid little number on the tag. In high school, I was always careful to hide the tag when shopping with friends because I was so embarrassed. I would've given anything to be an eight instead of a twelve.

I'd love to say I've outgrown that mindset. "We're more than a number!" - as the people say.

And most days, I believe it.

But we all have our moments.

One night, we went out to dinner for my birthday.

Instead of my usual end-of-day routine - laying on the couch in cozy clothes watching *The Office* - I made myself look nice. Shaved my legs. Washed the hair.

Pulled out the jeans.

I'd been working out regularly. Feeling strong. Semi-confident.

Hopeful, even.

And then I put them on.

They were tight.

Not *cute-tight*.

*Hard-to-breathe tight*.

And just like that, I went from feeling proud of myself to wanting to light those pants on fire.

And the annoying part?

I should know better.

Fifteen years ago, in the middle of my Renfrew days, a girl looked me dead in the eye and said, "Fuck the size of your jeans." She wasn't trying to be inspirational - she was just over it. And somehow, that blunt little pep talk gave me more confidence than any carefully worded affirmation ever has.

Back then, I believed her. I bought the ridiculous parachute pants. I felt freer, lighter, like maybe the number on the tag didn't get to boss me around anymore.

And yet here I am, standing in a parking lot with my tight jeans - realizing I'm still working on that same lesson. Still catching myself in the spiral and needing the reminder to let it go, loosen up, and stop letting an inch of denim decide how I feel about myself.

Fast forward to dinner, and it's all I can think about as I ate my salad with the cornbread croutons - possibly not helping things, but also... worth it.

### What am I doing wrong?

I've been eating better, working out, feeling good - and these jeans don't fit?

You know everything comes back to dog stuff for me, and this is no different.

Maybe you went on a walk with your dog, and they suddenly lost it on the neighbor's chihuahua - the one they've politely ignored for the past two months.

You've been *working* on this. Practicing. Watching all the videos. Showing up.

Shouldn't it be better by now?

And then the spiral starts:

*What am I doing wrong? Why can't I do this like other owners?*

When we got to the car, I told Bobby about my tight jeans and how uncomfortable I felt.

But the words "my jeans are too tight" weren't really about the jeans.

They were about:

I'm not working out enough.

I'm eating too much.

Why can't I have more discipline - like other people?

Bobby's response:

"Go ahead and unbutton them."

Right here? In the parking lot??

"Yeah. Why not?"

So I did.

All four buttons. Gone.

And immediately - I felt like myself again.

His solution wasn't to fix it or analyze it.

It was just... *let it go.*

Your dog slipping up doesn't mean you're not working hard.

And it doesn't mean you're behind or someone else would do this better. It might just mean... you need to loosen up on the story you're telling yourself. Because spoiler: no one else has it together either. They're just better at hiding the mess.

## 27 / COMPARISON

In today's world, it's so easy to compare. So it makes sense that it shows up here too - in the way we look at our dogs, our progress, and ourselves.

You'll be feeling pretty good about your body ... until you see someone's beach vacation and immediately start spiraling about your stomach.

You'll feel sure about your path ... until another pregnancy announcement shows up, and even if you didn't think you wanted kids, you suddenly feel like you're missing out.

And once you notice it in life, you start seeing it everywhere - especially in dog ownership.

You look around and think: Why is her dog so calm?

Why does their walk look so easy?

And why does my dog make literally *everything* harder than it should be?

Comparison creeps in fast.

And if you're not careful, it convinces you you're failing - even when you're *actually* doing what's best for you and your dog.

Example: I have a dog in for training who pulls really hard on walks, is reactive any time he sees a dog, and loses his mind over the doorbell.

He's also one of the sweetest dogs I've ever met.

He's a Goldendoodle - and whatever you think you know about doodles, this guy is rewriting the script.

Or maybe he's just leaning hard into his Golden Retriever side - the one that's more cozy-grandma-in-a-rocking-chair than restless chaos-in-fur.

Even with the reactivity, I'm seeing these glimpses of a softer dog underneath it all. Around the house, he's calm. Quiet. Content just being. That contrast is what makes him so interesting - and why I've been jokingly calling him a "unicorn dog." Not because he's perfect, but because he's reminding me that even the loudest dogs usually have a quieter side waiting to come out.

*He had an off switch.*

But just a few months ago, I worked with a dog who was the complete opposite.

No off switch.

If the unicorn dog could dial it down once he got home, this one didn't have a dial at all. He was on high volume all day, every day. Whining. Barking. Pacing. And the reactivity didn't stop on walks - it followed him everywhere. Was he sweet? Yes. But the kind of sweet that makes you question your sanity after the sixth meltdown before 10am.

My Oura ring kept alerting me that my stress levels were "elevated."

Oh, were they, Oura? Thanks for the update.

Because of that, the training process looked wildly different.

And that's probably why training your dog feels so different for you than it does for your Aunt Suzy - the one who loves to offer unsolicited advice from the comfort of her couch.

Or your friend whose dog basically trained himself - and who you love dearly but also kind of want to block on Instagram.

"Every dog is different" sounds so cliché, but I'm serious - I see it firsthand. All the time. And it's real.

Some dogs are so pushy, anxious, or draining that I find myself Googling things like "how to make money baking bread" or "grandma hobbies that double as a career."

Some dogs make me question if I want to keep training dogs.

And then - like the universe knows I need saving - I get a dog who reminds me why I fell in love with this work in the first place.

And it goes like that. Over and over.

But when it's just you and your dog?

When you're sitting alone in your house wondering why this feels so much harder than it should - it's almost too easy to compare.

It's too easy to scroll someone else's highlight reel and think:

"Why doesn't my dog act like that?"

One thing I find myself telling owners all the time is that I have experience to lean on because of all the different dogs I've worked with. You only have your dog. Of course it feels overwhelming sometimes. Because in a world where perfect walks and dreamy dogs flood our feeds, it's easy to forget that you're not behind. You're just figuring it out with a dog who clearly didn't come with an instruction manual.

I had to learn this as a trainer, too.

For me, it looked like learning to trust my instincts - not someone else's roadmap.

And one of the biggest things that helped me stop comparing?

Realizing that so much of the training journey comes down to who your dog *actually* is.

Not just what tools you're using or how consistent you are. But their temperament - the part no one really talks about until you're already in the thick of it.

That's where we're headed next. Because once you understand why your dog feels like more work than someone else's, everything gets a little easier to carry.

Don't get a dog unless you're open to the possibility that they won't be who you pictured - but exactly who you needed.

## 28 / NOT LIKE MY LAST DOG

> "That's when I want you to pause and ask: *what's the next right move?*" - me

For me, there are two types of dogs:

The one who loves everyone - you can drop them into a group and not worry about a thing.

And then the other one - reactive, fearful of people, or doesn't play well with others. The dogs who make you feel a little on edge because you're not sure what might happen next.

I've owned both.

And I'll be the first to say, having a dog who loves everyone is great.

It spoils you.

And honestly, it's almost worse if you've experienced the magic of a go-with-the-flow dog - because your next dog probably won't fit that mold.

And when that happens, you're left feeling... stumped.

When the stuff that worked before suddenly doesn't, that's when you start to unravel a bit.

That's when the doubt creeps in.

The regret.

The fear that it will always feel this hard.


But weirdly? That's where the real lessons sneak in - the kind you can't get from a YouTube video.

Bookmark this one for the "why can't my dog be normal?" days.


I was talking with an owner in a virtual coaching session. They had a six-month-old Australian Shepherd named Lucy, who just happened to be the total opposite of their last dog. "She was a lab and so laid back," the owner said. She was trying to smile through it.

I laughed a little, because I hear this all the time.

"But Lucy is the complete opposite. The only place she can relax is in her kennel."

Immediately, I thought of our German shepherd Louie.

I joked that Lou was the same, and I'm pretty sure she didn't lay down on her own until she was two.

The owner laughed and shot her husband a look that said oh no.

A look into their future.

"It's actually a great sign that Lucy relaxes in the kennel," I said. "It's her space to turn off that busy, working-dog brain."

I've found it's helpful to remind owners what kind of dog they have.

A working breed - like a shepherd or a collie - is not the same as your average doodle.

They need more from us.

And sometimes, it's just reassuring to hear why things might feel harder than expected.

(Side note: labs aren't always easy either.

One of the most challenging dogs I've ever worked with through my board and train program was a six-month-old chocolate labrador.

It always depends on the dog in front of you.)

We kept talking - about training, routines, stuff I'd recommend.

But more importantly, we talked about how she felt.

At one point, she said something that stuck out:

"Lucy reminds me of me. I think that's why this has been so hard - she's showing me the parts of myself I don't love."

This wasn't just about the dog.

"I felt the same way about Louie!" I said, almost shouting - like she'd just reassured me that *I* wasn't the only one.

I remember feeling like I was constantly hitting a wall with Louie.

I'm more of a couch potato - laid-back dog lady. Let's go for a casual walk and then binge Gilmore Girls under a cozy blanket.

Louie? She was a non-stop, go-go-go kind of dog.

And while I don't think I'm like that... I kind of am.

She was basically a walking version of my most anxious tendencies.

And I didn't want to deal with those parts of myself - so having a dog that mirrored them? Not fun.

One of the best things about struggling with your dog in ways you didn't expect? One day, you might be able to help someone else who's going through the same thing.

Anytime I find myself hitting a wall with a dog now, I remind myself: this will mean something one day.

"Okay, aside from the training stuff," I said, "I want you to start checking in with yourself when you're working with Lucy."

She tilted her head, listening.

"If you're feeling frustrated - or like you're trying to make progress in a session but keep getting stuck - that's your cue. That's when I want you to pause and ask: what's the next right move?

What can I do to reset?

Why am I feeling this way right now?"

Because here's the thing I've learned the hard way:

**Sometimes the dog who throws you for a loop ends up changing you the most.** They have a way of making you question everything you thought you knew. Suddenly, the skills and confidence you had with your last dog are non-existent. You second-guess your instincts. Compare everything.

And then you find yourself saying things like,

"I never had to do this with my last dog,"

as if that's helpful to anyone, especially you.

But that's the trap.

Thinking this dog should behave like that dog.

Thinking you should feel confident just because you did once.

But you're in new territory now.

And yeah, maybe it's louder, messier, and more confusing than you expected. But it's also where you start realizing you can handle way more than you give yourself credit for.

What if you stopped looking for the finish line altogether and just decided - this is your life with your dog - and you're going to make it a good one, even if it's not the one you pictured.

## 29 / BOX MIX BROWNIES AND SOURDOUGH STARTERS

Dog ownership isn't a "set it and forget it" thing. It's not a one-size-fits-all recipe. Some dogs are like those box-mix brownies. Simple. Sweet. You add a little structure, a few walks, some treats - and voilà. You've got yourself a well-behaved companion.

And then there are the dogs that feel more like sourdough starters.

High-maintenance. Unpredictable. The kind of dog that makes you question yourself, overthink every choice, sometimes collapse on the couch reminding yourself to just breathe.

But here's the thing about sourdough starters:

Once you figure out how to work with it - and keep it alive - it gives you something so good, so worth it, that all the trial and error almost doesn't matter.

It's the same with your dog.

It's about learning their recipe: temperament, genetics, breed, personality - all of it shapes who they are.

But the ingredient that makes the biggest difference?

You.

Your need for approval. The perfectionism. Keeping up appearances. Wanting life to fit in neat boxes.

When you get a dog who blows all of that up - the barking, the chaos, the total lack of chill - it might feel like everything you've spent your life trying to control is suddenly out in the open.

And maybe... that's not the worst thing.

Maybe it's the nudge you needed to stop making yourself smaller just so life feels tidy. To step into the room like you belong there. To stop softening your edges. And to drop the "polished" act.

Not just for them - but for you.

It's almost unfair - the stuff you've always been self-conscious about? They finally matter here.

Because with a dog who doesn't fit in, those exact parts of you are what make the difference. And maybe that's why these dogs find us - because they need an owner who also knows what it's like not to fit in.

## 30 / THE PERSONALITY PLOT TWIST

**Temperament** is the part of your dog's personality they were *born* with. The stuff you can train around, but not erase. Once I started paying attention to this piece, it made way more sense why some dogs are the life of the party, while others would rather skip the invite altogether.

It explains why two dogs in the same home can become best friends ... or start a fight in your living room.

Why one training plan feels like magic for one dog but like chaos for another.

And if your dog has ever made you want to pour a martini at 9am and look up "how to adopt a cat," - it could be a temperament thing.

Just like humans, dogs show up with their own personalities.

Their temperament shapes how they learn, how they push boundaries, and who they feel safe with.

Once you start recognizing who your dog is - instead of just what your dog does - everything shifts.

It changes how you train them - how you socialize them.

It even changes the way you set them up to succeed - in ways that finally feel like the *right* move.

And most importantly, it helps you let go of the guilt.

That creeping feeling that "another owner would do this better" starts to fade when you realize:

It's not just about being a good trainer or owner.

It's about understanding *who* you're training.

Over the years, I started noticing patterns - little clusters of personalities that kept showing up over and over again.

Not scientific, but - more like my own unofficial zodiac signs of the dog world.

(Type 3s, Virgos - you're safe here.)

As you read through them, see if you recognize a little bit of your dog in one - or maybe a mix of a few.

## 1. The Sensitive Dog

"I want to be brave, but the world feels so scary."

This dog feels everything deeply.

New places, fast movements, unfamiliar dogs - it's a lot.

They want to connect, but sometimes it's too much, too fast. They might come across as aloof or hesitant, but underneath it all, they're just trying to figure things out.

Sensitive dogs need calm leadership, slow introductions, and friends who respect their space.

Training with them is about building confidence – quietly and consistently - in small, safe steps.

## 2. The Strong Spirit

"If you don't lead, I will."

This dog knows exactly what they want - and they're not shy about it. High-energy, pushy, often rolling right over social cues like a bulldozer.

Without clear boundaries, chaos rules.

Strong Spirits thrive with structured, supervised socialization and calm, grounded dog friends who show them how to chill without leaning into their pushy energy and being picky about friends is crucial.

Training with them looks like: "I love your enthusiasm. Also, here's a boundary. (And another one.) (And another one.)"

## 3. The Steady Companion

"Where you go, I go."

This dog is the ride-or-die type.

Easygoing, sweet, happy to tag along wherever life takes them.

But - and this is important - they can sometimes get overshadowed by bigger personalities if you're not careful.

Steady Companions thrive when you gently build their independence, help them find their voice, and make sure they don't get steamrolled in social settings.

They don't need a lot of friends. They just need you.

### 4. The Fierce Protector

"I'll keep us safe, even if you don't need me to."

This dog sees everything.

Every new person, every minor disturbance that you probably missed.

They aren't trying to be difficult. They're trying to do their job: keeping their people safe.

Fierce Protectors thrive when you show them that you see what they see, but you've got it covered.

That they don't have to figure things out on their own.

Training with them is about giving them the relief of following your lead - instead of always trusting their own instincts first.

Seeing It In Real Life: Theo and Johnny

I've seen all of these types up close with my own dogs. Most recently, with Theo and Johnny.

Theo is a mix of Strong Spirit and Fierce Protector.

Johnny is the opposite - a Sensitive Soul and Steady Companion.

Before we adopted Johnny, I knew whoever came home had to get along with Theo.

(He's a mix of Rottweiler, German Shepherd, Belgian Malinois, and Pit Bull - at least according to the DNA test. Honestly, the second I saw "Malinois," his early days of trying to use us as chew toys made a lot more sense.)

From day one, his instincts to bite and protect were strong.

Over the years, he's softened - but he's still intense, just with boundaries now thanks to training.

And in true Fierce Protector form, his friend circle? Small but tight.

When I met Johnny at the shelter, I felt something different.

It wasn't his looks or breed that drew me in - it was his temperament.

Soft, nervous, calm - everything Theo wasn't.

Past Bethany might've picked a dog based on looks or vibes.

Now? It's all about personality.

When I reached out my hand and Johnny laid his head in my palm, it was a Sensitive Soul move if there ever was one.

It might sound strange, but dogs who do that?

Almost always more of a sensitive type.

When we brought Johnny home, we didn't just toss him into the backyard with our dogs and hope for the best.

We went for a walk.

Bobby walked Theo.

I walked Johnny.

Johnny inched closer, reading Theo's "don't mess with me" energy loud and clear.

Their conversation, if I had to translate:

Johnny: Hey! You seem cool. Can we hang out?

Theo: (growls) Don't get any closer. I don't know you.

Johnny: Oh - okay. Sorry.

Theo: (pretends Johnny doesn't exist.)

Inside, I was crying a little - wondering if Theo would ever like him - but I knew:

These things take time.

Each day, we circled the backyard like it was our personal dog track.

Theo following. Johnny staying polite.

By day five, I unclipped Johnny's leash.

Theo sniffed him. Johnny froze - classic Sensitive Soul - staring at the sky like maybe if he held still enough, he'd disappear.

"Let's go!" I said, breaking the tension.

We crossed the yard together - and then Theo did it:

A play bow.

Front paws stretched out, butt in the air - the universal dog signal for, "Okay, fine. You're cool."

That moment? It was the first sign this might work out after all.

I've found that a lot of owners have expectations for their dog based on who they want them to be - not who they actually are.

And that's totally normal.

If you haven't felt that at some point, you're probably not reading this book.

Because when you get the kind of dog you weren't expecting, you default to what you know.

Maybe it's the dog you grew up with.

Maybe it's the last dog you had who was basically a walking angel in fur.

So you start comparing.

Expecting similar results because it worked before.

But the thing that changes everything?

Personality.

You can't change who your dog is.

But you can learn how they're wired.

And when you do, you start making decisions that actually make sense for them.

You might even feel a little bit relieved.

Like:

"Ohhh. Kevin's a Strong Spirit. That's why this situation feels so hard for him."

It's not you.

It's not even something you have to fix.

It's just ... Kevin being Kevin.

And when you can meet Kevin where he is, instead of where you wish he was -

That's when everything starts to change.

Theo and Johnny

If you've built your identity around being easy and agreeable - then having a dog who challenges everything might be the thing that teaches you to take up space, speak up, and stop disappearing.

## 31 / SOMETIMES YOU JUST NEED A BREAK

THIS BITCH ISN'T MOVING. And neither am I.

One day after working with a particularly tough dog duo, I was so drained I caught myself fantasizing about my old life when I was a dog walker and pet sitter.

A time when I wasn't chasing big training goals or working through behavioral issues. Just walking dogs, sending cute photo updates, and living my best stress-free life.

(At least, that's how I remember it.)

For a few days, I let myself dream about it.

What if I just went back?

No behavior mod cases.

No reactivity drills.

Just leashes, sunshine, and happy little snapshots.

Then - as if the universe heard me - my neighbor walked past our house, "Hey! Do you know of a pet sitter?"

Um, what in the manifestation is happening right now?

I basically shouted, "I volunteer as tribute."

At first, it was perfect.

Beautiful lake view.

Chill vibes.

Little dog with big energy.

Exactly what I needed... for about five minutes.

Turns out Daisy had a few quirks.

Like eating wild mushrooms in the backyard.

(Magic mushrooms. Casual.)

Apparently, her owner had brushed it off with, "She's fine. The vet says it's not a big deal."

Meanwhile, I'm in the backyard with Daisy sprinting from shrub to shrub, trying to stop her from going full psychedelic at 9AM.

By visit two, I learned my lesson.

Harness on. Bribes ready.

I tried to follow the "only go right at the stop sign" rule from her owner's instructions.

But after the backyard mushroom chase, I made an executive decision:

We're going left.

Daisy hit the brakes and after a few minutes of standing in a silent standoff, I realized:

This bitch isn't moving. And neither am I.

We turned around and went home.

It hit me somewhere between the mushrooms and the stop sign:

I don't *actually* miss being a pet sitter.

I just needed a break.


If you're feeling drained, frustrated, or stuck with your dog right now?

Maybe you don't need to overhaul everything.

Maybe you just need a pause.

A day where you go for a walk just to walk - not to train.

An afternoon where you leave the leash in the closet and just exist together.

**Not every season has to be about progress.**

Sometimes the best thing you can do is step back, take a breath, and remember why you started in the first place.

Your dog will be okay.

And so will you.

## 32 / THE NAME GAME

It's Wednesday morning. I'm sitting in the kennel room with my chickens, and I start to panic.

I got six of them a few weeks ago, and until they're big enough for the coop, they're living in a bin in the corner of the kennel room - peeping away while I work.

My little grey chick, Winnie, is my favorite. She's the cuddliest of the six, and I swear - she really likes me.

The others look at me with bird-judgment. I can feel their skepticism.

They like me, sure - but not like Winnie.

And now I'm spiraling.

What if she's a rooster?

I'm not allowed to have roosters where I live.

So I jump straight to the ending:

She's a rooster.

I have to rehome her.

And when I do, I ugly cry.

Like hiccup-breathing cry.

I think back to when I was little - how I used to hiccup when I cried, which made me feel embarrassed.

So I'd hold my breath to hide it.

Which led to pitiful, gasping little hiccup-sobs.

Honestly, I should've just let it out.

And just like that, I'm back in the hospital room.

I'm watching the monitor - green waves, blue zigzags.

The green reminds me of a golf course.

The blue, of the ocean.

I try to imagine the beach. The sound of waves. The scratch of sand under my feet.

I look at my dad and think - how is this my life?

He was fine two days ago.

Now I'm back in the kennel room, with Winnie.

And I'm asking similar questions.

I never understood what heartbreak really was until I lost my dad.

And now, every time I worry that I'll lose something — anything - it's colored by that same tone.

Different, but familiar.

I'm in the van with Bobby, driving home from a road trip with our dogs. Johnny's in my lap and I start to quietly panic.

But I feel it so strongly, I assume my body's giving me away.

He was coughing after some zoomies at a rest stop.

What if it's heartworms?

He was tested, but what if it was a faulty test?

And just like that - I'm in the worst-case scenario.

What if he dies?

I start to cry silently.

Because - heartbreak.

Again.

Back to the hospital. It's nighttime.

A nurse comes in to check my dad's vitals.

She turns on the light while I lay on a cot in the corner.

"Joseph? Can you hear me? JOSEPH? Look over here, Joseph!"

Nobody called him that.

"It's Joe," I said. "Please call him Joe. That's what everyone calls him."

And then I'm back in the van.

With my grief dog.

The one I got to keep me from falling into a depression.

The one who makes me smile just by existing.

Now I'm back in the kennel room, with Winnie.

And I start naming the things around me.

Leashes.

Collars.

Green walls.

Wood panel.

Black bin.

Because heartbreak is something I can't control.

But I can try control where my thoughts go.


And this little game?

It works with dogs, too.

When you're in the thick of it - the barking at the window, the lunging on the leash, the pacing in their crate - your brain will sprint straight to "what if this never changes?"

It's loud, dramatic, and convinced it knows the ending.

So instead, bring yourself back to *right now*.

Name five things you can see.

Four things you can touch.

Three things you can hear.

It won't magically fix the moment, but it will stop your mind from living in the worst-case version of it.

And sometimes, that pause is all you need to take a breath, pick up the leash, and keep going.

## 33 / STRUCTURE IS CLARITY

There's this idea floating around that a dog with more freedom is automatically a happier dog.

It's why so many owners feel guilty about using a kennel - because letting a dog roam free in the house just seems nicer. Until the dog chews through the couch cushions or sneaks something dangerous out of the trash.

It's also why letting your dog sniff wherever they want on a walk is so widely encouraged - because we've been told that sniffing is natural and enriching, and putting rules on the walk somehow robs them of joy.

And listen - who doesn't want their dog to be happy?

Of course we do.

But here's the part that usually gets left out: That advice only works if your dog's already doing well.

It doesn't help when walks feel like chaos. When your arm is sore from leash pulling. When your nerves are shot from dodging triggers, or when your dog is barking and lunging and you're just trying to make it around the block without crying.

In those moments, letting your dog sniff for as long as they want doesn't feel enriching.

It feels exhausting.

So let's say this out loud:

How you feel on the walk matters, too.

Adding structure to the walk - like teaching a heel command, or setting clearer boundaries around when sniffing is allowed - doesn't mean you're being controlling. It means you're creating a shared rhythm. One where your dog can settle in and follow your lead. One where you can enjoy the time shared with your dog.

Some dogs need more boundaries than others.

And that's not bad. It's just how things go sometimes.


Here are a few examples of when one dog can, and another can't - and why that's okay:


- Johnny can cuddle on the couch with me. I love it. But our dog Theo can't - because he growls when we ask him to move. And I don't want to reward that kind of behavior with a big privilege like couch time.

- Susie can have more freedom to sniff on walks. She's sweet, not reactive, and sticks close to her owner. But Tank? If he pulls to sniff, he starts thinking he can pull toward anything - including the next dog he wants to bark at. Clear structure helps him stay grounded, and he's still allowed sniff breaks - but they happen when his owner says "break."

•Nellie can greet guests at the door. She's polite and calm and then walks away. But when Harvey greets guests, he jumps, barks, and spins in circles. So, for him, the doorbell means going to place (the place command). It helps him settle his nervous system and not overwhelm visitors - or himself.

•Daisy can eat out of a slow feeder on a mat near the other dogs. She's relaxed around food. But Max guards his bowl if anyone comes near. So he eats all his meals in his crate - and that makes everyone feel safer.

•Louie can be off-leash at the park. He has a solid recall and checks in constantly. But Benny sees a squirrel and it's game over. So he wears a long line for more freedom with safety. No shame in that - it's what helps him succeed.

•Maple can stay out while her owners run errands. She naps by the window. But Goose? Goose shreds the blinds and paces the hallway. So he hangs in the crate when they leave, and it's been the best thing for him (and their living room).

If you're not sure what structure might look like for your dog, think of it like giving your dog a "job." It gives them clear direction, a way to channel themselves in moments when their instincts want to do something primal that doesn't exactly fit in suburbia (like chasing squirrels, guarding the sidewalk, or redecorating your couch cushions). A job doesn't mean they're clocking in at 9am, it just means you're giving their brain and body a clear role in the moment. For me, that looks like: "kennel" for crate time, "heel" on our walks, a "place" command in the house, "down" when we're out and about, and a reliable recall.

Each one offers clear direction.

Each one says, I've got you. You're not in this alone.

And in a busy, unpredictable world, that clarity is a gift - not just for your dog, but for you, too.

And here's the part I wish more owners knew: structure isn't just about making things less chaotic. It's also how you can help your dog become more confident. One of my go-to formulas with nervous dogs is simple job + a little exposure = confidence over time. Give them something to do (heel on a walk, place at home) and then start to add in some challenges. Not a flood of new experiences, just short sessions, little nudges, small wins. That's how confidence stacks up - not with dramatic breakthroughs, but with the boring stuff you do again and again.

And when you look at it that way, structure doesn't feel like taking something away from your dog. It feels like giving both of you a little breathing room. Less chaos. More calm. The kind of walk where you finally get to enjoy each other instead of just surviving the block.

Structure isn't punishment. It's what gives your dog clarity and gives *you* peace of mind.

Working with dogs reminds me of growing my little garden. (Yes, I've entered my gardening era. Blame sourdough.) You plant a tiny starter. You water it every morning. You stare at it like a weirdo, hoping for growth you can't see just yet. And then one morning - not in a rush, or some big dramatic reveal - there it is. A tiny green bud. Proof that everything you were doing mattered. It's quiet, and almost too easy to miss. But it's the slow kind of magic you only get to see if you're willing to wait for it.

## 34 / GLIMMERS

Will my dog always be like this?

There will be days when you feel like you're witnessing a forever problem in the making.

I felt that way a lot in those first few weeks with Johnny, catching myself overanalyzing little things and worrying they'd turn into bigger problems.

Like, anytime we got in the pool, he'd run and hide in the bushes. Or, whenever he saw a person on the walk he'd try and run back to our house.

But day by day, week by week, Johnny started showing me little glimmers of progress.

Small moments that gave me hope.

Have you ever heard the 3-3-3 rule? It's something that tends to float around the dog world as a guideline for when you bring home a new dog:

three days to decompress,

three weeks to start settling in,

three months to feel at home.

And I'm here to say - there's something to it.

But I also think training, or structure, helps.

The thing I want you to remember is that one moment doesn't define who your dog is. Whether you just brought a dog home and feel overwhelmed by the new things you're noticing, or you've had your dog for a while and new issues are popping up -

When you start to overthink it, remember:

it's just a moment.

It doesn't mean your dog will be like this forever.

I kept waiting for that "everything clicks" moment with Johnny - the moment that told me, Okay, we're going to be fine. And it didn't happen in a big, dramatic way.

It happened one morning on a walk in our neighborhood. The same route we took every day. I remember hoping our neighbor Luke would be outside, tinkering in his yard. He's an older, retired veteran - one of those guys who seems a little salty at first, but you quickly learn he's quite the softie.

A few months earlier, when we stopped to say hello, Johnny freaked out and tried to bolt. I had to give my standard spiel: "He's nervous with new people. If you just ignore him, he'll be okay."

Luke showed me a photo of his childhood dog from the farm. She was black with a big white spot over one eye. He talked about how much he loved dogs. I could tell he wanted Johnny to like him. And I did, too.

So, on this particular walk - months later - I saw a glimmer.

Luke stepped out of his garage like always. And Johnny just... sat next to me.

No drama.

No "holy shit, who's this person" energy.

Just existed.

And I couldn't believe it.

That's when I knew:

We were finding our rhythm.

Not perfectly or instantly. But it was happening.

So if you're in the thick of it, wondering when it'll start to feel easier - remember: A bad moment doesn't mean your dog will always be that way. It just means you're both still learning - and progress is already happening, even if it's quieter than you expected.

A picture of Luke's childhood dog.

No one prepares you for the hard parts of dog ownership. But no one tells you how much they'll change you either.

## 35 / EMPATHY

EVERY CAMPSITE WAS BOOKED. We were tired, a little crunchy around the edges, and weighing our options when a couple in the same exact van as us waved us down and offered to share their spot.

They noticed one of our dogs peaking their head out of the window and the woman's face shifted - like the invitation had just gotten a little more complicated.

"But we have a dog," the woman said quickly. "She's older and doesn't like other dogs."

I recognized something in her voice - the quiet fear of what might happen if things went wrong.

That mix of preemptive shame and the hope that we'd understand.

And I *did*.

Because I've been that owner. The one who walks into a new space already scanning for exits. The one who explains her dog's issues with a nervous laugh, even though none of it feels funny.

And the one with four dogs crammed into our van - half of them not thrilled about other dogs either.

I told her not to worry.

We'd keep our distance.

I watched her shoulders drop a little. Her dog stayed close. Ours quiet in the van. It was uneventful in the best way.

And it stuck with me.

Because there was a time - before I had *those* dogs - when I might've quietly judged someone like her.

Not intentionally.

But I would've had opinions.

Like, *Why bring your dog if they can't handle this?* Like the Home Depot guy.

Or *That would never happen with my dog.*

But the thing is... once you've been humbled by owning a challenging dog, you stop thinking in hot takes.

You learn to see people where they are.

And you stop assuming every reactive dog is "bad" or that every overwhelmed owner is doing something wrong.

And you start recognizing the courage it takes just to *show up* - to go on the walk, book the trip, take up space - even when things are hard.

Because when you've had *that* kind of dog, you know that

showing up doesn't always mean confident walks and dog friendly greetings. Sometimes it just means trying again.

And making the best of it.

That woman and I didn't talk long.

But I saw her.

And I think - maybe - she saw me too.

Turns out, surviving the hard parts of dog ownership makes you the exact kind of person someone else hopes they'll run into.

Because empathy like that? You only earn it by going through it.

## 36 / CLIMBING TO NOWHERE

About a month after my dad passed away, I decided to take working out seriously.

I wanted to get into the best shape of my life.

Can you hear the drama in that?

"Best shape of my life!"

Like I'm auditioning for a Nike commercial.

But I'm an all-or-nothing kind of girl.

I love a good challenge.

It started when I found one of my dad's old journals and a particular entry stuck out.

It's from when I was in high school.

"Bumps just got back from a run. She looked so strong and happy."

My dad never really commented on how I looked - not in that way. Sure, he called me beautiful and said sweet things.

But "strong and happy"? That was different.

Reading that note - how he saw me that day - made me smile.

He sounded proud. And something about those words - *strong and happy* - made me want to become that again.

For both of us.

I start googling personal trainers the same way overwhelmed dog owners search for help. And almost like it was meant to be, I find someone.

I recognized her from my days working at the Tropical Smoothie in the YMCA. Red hair. Muscles you could see from across the gym.

One time, I overheard her telling a client to get the sushi from Whole Foods. "It's made with brown rice," she said. "A much better choice."

So even though I barely had enough money for gas - let alone sushi from the fancy grocery store - I drove out of my way to get it. *Maybe this was the secret to a great body*.

Pretty sure I overdrafted my account.

So yeah. Finding her again felt like a sign and I booked a session for the next morning.


It didn't take long for me to learn that her training style was... intense.

High intensity. All the time.

She starts me on the Stairmaster to warm up and yells across the gym: "Faster! There's no room for easy in this gym!"

I watch two women across the room doing some kind of leisurely ab thing on a yoga ball with another trainer and I wish I was them. But here I am. Sweating. Gasping for breath. Climbing to nowhere. And wondering what the hell I got myself into.

I'm ready to quit - until something strange happens.

Brenda puts me on one of her old school cycle bikes and cranks the resistance - making me pedal like my life depends on it.

After about thirty minutes when I think I can't go any further, I look over and - I swear - I see my dad riding next to me.

He's younger. Smiling. Cheering me on.

That's why I stay.

And why, in some demented way, I almost look forward to going. I want to see my dad.

A few weeks later, Bobby and I show up for a weigh-in. It's Brenda's New Year Challenge - one of the reasons I was most excited to sign up with her. The prize is $500 and my competitive side is peaking.

I'm nervous because I hate getting on a scale. And with someone who says "no excuses" like it's a personality?

Hate this. So much.

We walk to the back toward her office, and I still have my purse on. Brenda snaps: "Take off that fucking purse. You can't have that on back here."

And for some reason, on that day, her harshness hit different.

I felt like I twelve again. Small. Exposed. Like I did something wrong just by existing.

I walk out without saying a word. Embarrassed. Upset I didn't stand up for myself. But something about Brenda makes me feel so dumb. Like I'm constantly trying to earn her approval - and never quite getting there.

I want her to say something like, "Good job!" or, "Proud of you! You're looking strong today."

Things my dad would say.

I miss his support more than anything.

That day reminds me of a younger version of myself - the one who never stood up for herself. The one who always stayed quiet to stay safe.

But I'm not her anymore.

Becoming a dog trainer changed that.

Because when you work with dogs who need you to speak up for them, you get a little braver about using your voice everywhere else, too.

We still had another month paid at Brenda's gym, but I was done.

As much as I wanted to feel strong and happy, working out with her made me feel the opposite.

I used to think strength meant pushing through, no matter what.

But I've learned that real strength is quieter than that.

It's knowing when something's no longer serving you.

It's choosing what you know is best over approval. No matter what anyone else thinks.

And sometimes, it's walking away - whether it's from a trainer who makes you feel small, a version of yourself who doesn't yet know you deserve better, or a situation with your dog that you realize isn't fair to either of you. Walking away doesn't always mean giving up. Sometimes it means choosing the harder kind of love - the kind that makes space for something better.

Letting go isn't the opposite of love.

Sometimes, it's the proof of it.

## 37 / WHEN THE HARDEST CHOICE IS THE RIGHT ONE

The call came before sunrise.

Three missed calls. Two voicemails.

Owners I loved working with.

His voice, shaky.

"There was a fight. Sarah's in the hospital. She got bit."

Sarah was the kind of owner every dog deserves.

The one who asks all the right questions.

Follows through on every piece of advice.

Gives it her all.

And now she was sitting in a hospital room because of a single piece of food that hit the floor.

I drove to their house in the dark - mind racing.

When I got there, Willow was curled up in her kennel.

There was blood on her paws.

She looked up at me - tired, a little nervous, but still the beautiful dog I remember.

I loaded her into my van.

The car ride to the vet felt endless.

Willow stared at me with her flecked hazel-blue eyes, and I cried behind the steering wheel.

She had gone through my board and train program just a few months earlier.

She was doing so well.

Until now.

Later that afternoon, Sarah and John came to pick her up.

Both looked like they hadn't slept in days.

Standing in my driveway, listening to them try to figure out what came next,

I realized something I wasn't ready to admit:

Sometimes love isn't enough to make it work.

John loved their other dog, Rose - the sweet, easygoing Lab mix.

And he was scared that keeping Willow meant risking Rose.

Sarah wasn't just committed - she adored Willow through all the messy, complicated parts.

But they weren't on the same page anymore.

And it wasn't because they didn't care.

It wasn't because they weren't trying hard enough.

It was because sometimes, a dog just isn't the right fit - no matter how much you want them to be.

But I couldn't stop myself.

"But ... what about Willow?"

The words barely left my mouth before I got choked up.

And I wished I could take them back.

Because this isn't my dog.

This isn't my life.

They had both tried so hard.

And it still wasn't a good fit.

We kept in touch, and I later found out they re-homed Willow.

Sarah texted me - "It's the perfect home for her. I'm so grateful we were able to find them."

I wanted to be relieved.

Sarah was happy. Willow was in the right home. It all worked out.

But for a long time, I couldn't shake the feeling that I had failed.

Because isn't that the goal? To make it work. To fix the problem?

We don't talk about it enough, but here's the truth: sometimes keeping a dog isn't what's best for them. Sometimes the bravest choice is also the most heartbreaking one - giving them a different home.

If that's part of your story, it doesn't erase the love you had or the effort you gave. It just means you loved them enough to choose what they needed over what you wanted. That isn't failure. That's the kind of love no one talks about - *the kind that costs you something.*

## 38 / THE THING ABOUT TIME

I WAS SITTING on the couch with Bobby. The TV was on but muted, our dinner plates still on the coffee table between us. I remember picking at the crust of my pizza, feeling that restless mix of hope and uncertainty in my chest.

"What if I could help owners like me one day?" I said, half testing the words, half daring him to tell me it was ridiculous.

He didn't. He just looked at me for a second, like he could see I meant it.

And that was it - the conversation that started everything.

Six months later, I flew across the country to attend a seminar hosted by the very trainers I'd been binging on YouTube. It was an investment we couldn't really afford - but we took the leap anyway. Being around other aspiring dog trainers felt like someone had handed me a map I didn't know I needed. I came home lit up, ready to try everything I'd learned with Theo.

I kept walking dogs, but I started asking their owners if I could train with them, too. Some said yes, and I'd post little videos online and people started reaching out for help. I couldn't believe it. And about three months later, I got my first board and train client. That's when I let my pet-sitting clients know I wouldn't be able to walk their dogs anymore.

It was bittersweet, and I knew I'd miss the dogs I saw every day, but I was so motivated to help owners who were where I'd been - overwhelmed and in need of some hope.

I wanted to go all in.

That leap - from scared owner to brand-new trainer - turned into something I never could've pictured that night on the couch. Eight years later, I co-created a training seminar with my best friend, The Trainer In You. We built what we wished we'd had, added our own flavor, and turned it into a community of female dog trainers who have found their people and cheer each other on from all across the country. It's what we dreamed of - but back then, I couldn't have imagined just how good it would feel to be here.

That's the thing about time - it has a way of showing you what all those little steps were building toward. You don't always see it when you're in the middle of it, but looking back, you realize just how far you've come.

---

My face was hot and it felt like my heart was pounding in my throat.

I was sure they could all see how nervous I was.

. . .

I'm lying on a lounge chair in my friend's backyard. We just arrived to prep for our first Trainer In You seminar for dog trainers the following day. And I was spiraling.

So, I called my dad.

"We just finished clearing out Marsha's house - so many things," he said. His sister passed away the week before.

"This was a workout," he added, sounding exhausted but upbeat. That was his gift. He could turn grief into something grounding. Not in a toxic positivity way - just real. Good.

"Bumps," he said, and I could hear something coming. He always called me Bumps when he had something he really wanted me to hear.

"I want us to think about this when we get down on ourselves. One day you're alive and vibrant, and the next your family is cleaning out your house. I don't want to waste time on things that don't matter. Let's get the most out of this life."

It was the perfect motivational-dad moment.

I took a breath. "I'm just... so nervous about tomorrow. What if they don't like it? What if I'm terrible at this?"

He didn't skip a beat.

"Oh, I totally get that. That's scary. But Bumps - it's not about you. It's about them. Focus on how you can help them. You can't go wrong when you do that."

. . .

—

Two years later, I'm in my living room.

Ten dog trainers are looking back at us. It's our third time hosting The Trainer In You.

My dad passed away six months ago.

There's a framed print on the wall to my left – it was my dad's.

Joe DiMaggio swinging a bat, a crowd cheering behind him.

My dad's name is Joe.

I feel the pinch from the small pin on my calf that's pinned to my pants. One of his old coworkers had them made. It says:

"Jojo, always with us."

And beneath that:

INTEGRITY. HONESTY.

I whisper it to myself, over and over.

It's not about you. It's about them.

About them. Not you.

Breathe in - Joe. Baseball.

Breathe out - you can do this.

I was holding a lot that day.

Grief, mostly. The kind that sneaks up on you when you're

trying to focus. And nerves, too - the shaky, hot kind that makes your voice feel too small for the room.

I wanted to seem steady.

Like I wasn't falling apart. Like I could still lead the room the way he'd want me to.

I thought if I looked the part, no one would question me.

But the truth was - I was questioning myself.

Not just as a speaker, but as a person. As a daughter missing her dad. As someone trying to hold it together and show up anyway.

And that pressure to hold it together?

That part I think you understand, too.

You want to seem like a good owner.

Like your dog's behavior is under control.

Like you know what you're doing.

But sometimes all that pressure to get it right gets in the way of actually being present.

It's not about being perfect or never doubting yourself.

It's just... can you be honest with yourself? And still keep showing up?

And if the answer's no today - that's okay too.

You can try again tomorrow.

It's never about one moment, one seminar, or one perfectly trained dog. It's about stringing together all those shaky steps, all those "try again tomorrow" days, until one day you look back and realize you've built something you never thought you could.

Because that's what this whole journey really is - a practice in becoming.

## 39 / HOW'S THAT WORKING FOR YOU?

> "A seed has to destroy itself for the flower to bloom ... your life can't change if you don't change." - from my dad's notes

GROWING UP, my parents loved Dr. Phil, and my dad especially loved to drop his well-known tagline anytime he wanted to drive a point home or wrap up a story with dramatic flair:

"How's that working for you?"

And as much as I cringe at quoting a daytime TV host - it's a little too perfect not to.

Because no matter what's going on with you and your dog - no matter how different it looks from what other people are doing - you can always ask: How's that working for me?

It's something I say to owners all the time when we're coming up with a plan to work through a problem behavior like reactivity or anxiety: Try it. And if it doesn't work, we can try something else.

It's really that simple.

Nothing is forever.

Not the rules or the structure.

You can always pivot.

You're not signing a lifelong contract every time you try something new. Try it. Adjust it. Scrap it completely and start fresh tomorrow.

And honestly?

That's usually when the good stuff finally shows up.

Not when you're white-knuckling some perfect plan you heard on Instagram, but when you exhale, look at your dog, and go - okay, what do we *actually* need today?

That's when it starts to click.

When you stop chasing what's "supposed to work" and start noticing what actually works.

When you loosen the reins just enough to see the dog in front of you.

So yeah - turns out, progress doesn't always look like what the internet said it would.

Sometimes it looks like breaking your own rules.

Or letting your dog take up space on the couch.

Or saying "screw it" and tossing them a french fry.

It looks like trusting yourself, even when it doesn't look like what anyone else is doing.

Forget what you're "supposed" to do. The better question is always: Is this working for me and my dog?

Because that's the point - figuring out what works for you, your dog, and your life.

Sometimes that means letting go of what you thought it *had* to look like - and being open to something different.

As my dad once wrote -

*A seed has to destroy itself for the flower to bloom.*

Sometimes, it's not about becoming someone else.

It's about shedding what's not working - so the real stuff has space to grow.

I didn't get the dog

who made me feel ready.

I got the one who made

me *become* ready.

## 40 / FROM THE FLOOR TO HERE

I'M STANDING in our kitchen on a Saturday. We made homemade pizza. My family's in town - brother, sister-in-law, niece, and nephew.

The oven lets out a cloud of steam as I pull out the margarita pizza my niece, Adelaide, made.

I glance over and see my brother playing with Theo.

The dog I almost took back to the shelter.

The one who left me in tears, wondering if I could really do this.

But here, in this moment, he's the reason everyone is smiling.

I watch my brother laugh and he reminds me so much of my dad.

I miss him.

And I'm grateful - grateful for Theo and everything he's taught me.

Grateful for family that makes it feel like my dad is still in the room.

The next morning, I drive over to say goodbye before they head back to Georgia. As I pull up to park, I glance at the time:

11:14.

The date of my dad's passing - 11/14.

I sit there for a minute, just staring at the clock - missing him and somehow still feeling lucky.

Some losses never stop hurting.

But life keeps finding ways to hand me pieces of him -

In a laugh that sounds like his, a dog who changed everything, a family that feels like home.

And I think -

Maybe that's what healing really is.

Not the absence of pain, but the presence of love - mixed into the small, ordinary moments we get to keep.

I think back to the version of myself who laid on the bedroom floor, convinced she wasn't cut out for this. The one who thought she'd made a mistake.

I didn't know it then, but that moment - the one that felt like an ending - was really the start of everything that matters to me now.

Because Theo - the dog I almost let slip away - was the beginning of the life I didn't know I was building.

If you're somewhere in the thick of it right now - wondering if you can do this, wondering if you've made a mistake - I hope you keep going. Because the struggle isn't the end of your story. It's the start of a new one.

Theo - the dog who changed everything.

**Dear Owner,**

When you get the dog you didn't expect, life might feel messier than you signed up for. But I hope you can believe - even if it's not today or next week - that this dog might be the thing you needed all along.

And that when you think back on this season, you won't just remember the frustration or the chaos. You'll remember the ways you grew without realizing it - the boundaries you learned to set, the voice you learned to use, the parts of yourself you didn't even know were there until your dog gave you a reason to find them.

Because the gift of the dog you didn't expect isn't just who they become. It's who you become because of them.

Love, Bethany

P.S. It's not just you.

## ABOUT THE AUTHOR

Bethany Johnson is a professional dog trainer and writer who has spent the past decade helping owners navigate the messy, beautiful reality of life with challenging dogs. Through her business, Walking Dog Training, she has supported thousands of dog owners with guides, coaching, and online resources that focus on more than just obedience - they focus on the person holding the leash.

Bethany wrote *Dear Owner* for anyone who has ever felt like they weren't cut out for the dog in front of them. Her work blends honest storytelling with practical encouragement, reminding owners that their worth isn't defined by their dog's behavior, but by the strength they uncover in the process.

When she isn't training dogs or writing, Bethany can be found in her backyard garden, baking sourdough, or wrangling her small flock of chickens. She lives in Orlando, Florida, with her husband, Bobby, and their four dogs.

/ ABOUT THE AUTHOR

Find more of her work at walkingdogtraining.com or on Instagram @walkingdogtraining